Oral History

A Reference Guide
and Annotated Bibliography

by

Patricia Pate Havlice

McFarland & Company, Inc., Publishers
Jefferson, N.C., & London

Library of Congress Cataloging in Publication Data

Havlice, Patricia Pate.
  Oral history.

  Bibliography: p.
  Includes index.
  1. Oral history — Bibliography. I. Title.
Z6201.H38 1985 [D16.14]   016.907'2   84-43227

ISBN 0-89950-138-9

Printed in the United States of America

McFarland Box 611 Jefferson NC 28640

Table of Contents

Acknowledgments

I would like to thank Patricia Garrett and her reference staff at the University of Houston–Clear Lake campus for designing and executing computer searches. Gay Carter and Deirdre Becker made suggestions and helped me decipher codes used by various publications. At the Freeman Memorial Library, Gloria Wells did yeowoman service in getting interlibrary loan material. From the far reaches of Belmont, Massachusetts, and Batavia, Illinois, respectively, Mary Claire Walsh Phelan and Sally Bast sent photocopies of regional periodical articles.

Introduction

The modern oral history movement began with Allan Nevins' work at Columbia University after World War II. For at least the previous decade he had been concerned with the amount of material which was being lost to history because fewer people were putting their thoughts on paper. With a graduate student he began a program to record interviews with prominent men in longhand. Acquisition of a wire recorder speeded the work and the advent of the modern tape recorder reeled the movement into the modern age. The university's Oral History Research Office set the standard and is emulated across the country and around the world today.

As the equipment for doing interviews became accessible and simpler to operate and knowledge of the discipline spread, changes in the focus and purpose of programs came about. Nevins set out originally to capture for posterity the thoughts of "great men" and their motives for behaving as they had. He wanted a record to replace diaries which were no longer being kept: he probed for significant information which would be stored away for the use of future historians. He let his speakers place restrictions on who could use the transcripts; tapes were destroyed when transcribing was completed.

Alex Haley's phenomenal **Roots** sent people off to look for theirs and in the course of searching many hit on the idea of tape recording the reminiscences of older members of the family. In Rabun, Georgia, Eliot Wigginton began Foxfire, a project implemented by his high school students to record the culture and character of a rural area.

From college to home to community the oral history movement developed, until Cheshire-like, it came to mean whatever the speaker wanted it to mean. By 1983 it metamorphosized into distinct forms; cultural journalism denotes its use in classroom settings as lagniappe; the life history of the "ungreat" is important to friends and relatives; and

1

the rigorously defined programs of the University of California's Regional Oral History Office carry out Nevins' ideal.
This bibliography is a record of the growth and changes
which took place over the last three decades.

Reference Guide

This volume brings together under one cover a listing
of books, articles and dissertations on oral history which
appeared in print from the 1950's to late 1983. The annotations
which accompany almost every reference are descriptive
summaries of the contents. In a few instances work which
is especially helpful to the beginner or which is particularly
well done is noted. I noted reviews for books which were
unobtainable by my deadline.

The bibliography was compiled from a variety of sources.
Several yielded a large number of titles. For those who wish
to add to this compilation the following reference tools
will be most helpful.

Bibliographic Sources

The largest number of references, many of which were
not duplicated in other sources, came from **America: History
and Life** and **Historical Abstracts**. The ABC-Clio publications
were searched by the computerized index service DIALOG
which can be inexpensively accessed if the user specifies
the option of having only the abstract number printed out.
Once the numbers are in hand sitting down at the index
tables and reading through the abstracts is simple.

The slightly peculiar indexing of **Dissertation Abstracts**
was the source of the dissertations listed here. I concentrated
on those which used oral history as a method of research,
excluding those which relied for data on interviews. For
the convenience of those wanting to read the abstract or
needing ordering information, I noted the volume and page
of the abstract.

Another major source of references was the American
Historical Association's **Writings on American History: A
Subject Bibliography of Articles.** Beginning with the 1962-73
cumulation there is a separate section for oral history materials. Many interview transcripts, most of them not listed
elsewhere, occur here. Articles dealing with oral tradition
in its most narrow sense are also included.

In the Folklore section of the Modern Language Association's annual bibliography some fugitive references were gleaned. The problem with this source is that a zealous indexer saw the words "oral history" in the article and placed it here when in reality the author barely touched on the concept.

There are four places to look for references to oral history books: **American Book Publishing Record; Cumulative Book Index; The British National Bibliography; Library of Congress Catalog, Books: Subjects.** All are serial bibliographies with excellent indexing. Check for titles as well as subjects in the first three for the most complete coverage. Searching all four is not totally redundant.

Continuing indexes put out by H.W. Wilson such as **Reader's Guide, Education Index, Social Sciences Index, Public Affairs Information Service,** and **Essay and General Literature Index** turned up many articles and some books on both popular and specialized levels.

Since 1976 ERIC has used "oral history" as a descriptor. Its companion **Current Index to Journals in Education** yielded references not duplicated in **Education Index.** Books which I located through ERIC are distinguishable by the abstract number (ED followed by six digits).

Magazine Index, the microfilm bibliography, put out by Information Access Company has popular material, much of it with a regional slant not found in the Wilson publications. That strength can be frustrating to the user seeking an article in a periodical such as **Boston** or **Chicago** and too pressed for time to wait for a photocopy via interlibrary loan.

After searching several newspaper indexes including those for the **Christian Science Monitor** and the **Wall Street Journal** I would recommend using the **New York Times Index.** It is a good place to look for material concerning the New York City area and does a fair job of locating information on Connecticut and New Jersey as well. The letters s, m and l which accompany page citations to articles stand for (quick, take a wild guess) short, medium and long, indicating the approximate wordage.

Because libraries are a main depository of oral history material both **Library Literature** and **Library and Information Science Abstracts** should be searched. I did not include in my bibliography announcements of the opening of new archives or additions to existing collections but anyone looking for that type of information should search these two indexes.

Since 1970 the **National Union Catalog of Manuscript Collections** has included a special index listing interview transcripts and collections of sound recordings. The fifth edition of Lee Ash's **Subject Collections** (Bowker, 1978) lists oral history collections in the U.S. and Canada.

Journals

Several journals whose main focus is oral history were born in the last few years. **Oral History Review** began in 1973 and is a continuation of the Oral History Association's **Proceedings** of the Annual Colloquia. It is indexed in **America: History and Life** and **Historical Abstracts.** Articles on oral history are its main staple but it also includes book reviews, notices of association business, and specialized bibliographies. Bill Katz, **Library Journal**'s resident periodical critic, wrote favorably of it in the August, 1980 issue (p. 1616). For subscription information write to:

Oral History Association
Box 13734
North Texas State University
Denton, TX 76203

The Oral History Society, a British group, publishes **Oral History** which began in 1969 and is indexed in the ABC-Clio guides. Its main focus is work in Great Britain but it has also published in English the work of Continental oral historians. The group's address:

University of Sussex
Dept. of Sociology
Oral History Society
Wivenhoe Park
Colchester, England

Our bilingual neighbors to the north put out the **Canadian Oral History Association Journal.** Begun in 1975 as an annual it now publishes two numbers a year. Articles in French and English with a Canadian slant, book reviews and general news are included. Abstracted in the ABC-Clio indexes.

Canadian Oral History Association
P.O. Box 301
Station A
Ottawa, Ontario, Canada K1N 8V3

The **International Journal of Oral History,** begun in 1980, appears thrice yearly. Its scope is world wide. It is indexed in **Current Contents** as well as being abstracted in **America: History and Life** and **Historical Abstracts.**

Meckler Books
520 Riverside Ave.
P.O. Box 405
Saugatuck Station
Westport, Conn. 06880

Frontiers, a feminist periodical on a scholarly plane, devoted its Summer, 1977, issue to women's oral history. It contained excerpts of interviews, articles on life history and family history.

Colloquia

I have not listed the publications of the annual colloquia held by the Oral History Association in the bibliography. Summaries of the proceedings were written up by various participants who often included their own opinions on what took place. Look in the index of this volume under the subject heading "Colloquia" for these articles.

The main entry for published colloquia is National Colloquium on Oral History. The individual titles are:

Oral History at Arrowhead. Edited by Elizabeth I. Dixon and James V. Mink. September 25-28, 1966. Papers by James V. Mink, Elizabeth I. Dixon, Allan Nevins, Louis Shore, Donald J. Schippers and Gould P. Colman.

The Second National Colloquium on Oral History. Edited by Louis M. Starr. November 18-21, 1967. Papers by Alfred A. Knopf, Donald J. Shippers, E. Douglas Hamilton, Philip A. Crowl, Forrest C. Pogue and Luther H. Evans.

The Third National Colloquium on Oral History. November 22-25, 1968. Edited by Gould P. Colman. Papers by Louis M. Starr, Walter Lord, Philip Crowl, Charles Morrissey, William Manchester, Knox Mellon, Joe B. Frantz, Elizabeth Mason, John F. Stewart and James B. Rhoads.

The Fourth National Colloquium on Oral History. Edited by Gould P. Colman. November 7-10, 1969. Papers by Elie Abel, Forrest C. Pogue, Peter D. Olch, Barbara Tuchman, and about two dozen others.

Selections from the Fifth and Sixth National Colloquia on Oral History. November 13-16, 1970 and October 8-10,

1971. Edited by Peter D. Olch and Forrest C. Pogue. Papers by T. Harry Williams, James MacGregor Burns, and several others. Abstracted in ERIC: ED 074 544. Colloquia held after this date are noted in issues of the **Oral History Review.**

Subject Headings

The headings in the index are those which I think will be most useful to the user. Rather than making "oral history" a heading with several subdivisions I opted for the following:

Bibliography

Catalogs

Classroom—subdivided by level; elementary, high school and college

Cultural journalism—for information on community projects

Development—deals with the history of the movement, primarily with events and personalities since World War II

Editing process

Equipment

Genealogy—making a record of family history

Legal aspects—the rights of the interviewee

Libraries and archives

Methodology—doing a project from idea to transcription

The Bibliography

Bibliographies of Oral History

1 Anderson, R. Wayne. "Oral History Dissertations, 1977-81." **Oral History Review** 10 (1982), 133-144. Dissertations on oral history methodology and those which make extensive use of interviews are noted by Anderson.

2 Bornat, Joanna. "Women's History and Oral History: An Outline Bibliography." **Oral History** 5 (Autumn 1977), 124-135. Sociological investigation, anthropology and autobiography are the three main types of books which comprise this bibliographic essay.

3 Evans, Frank B. "Oral History." In **Modern Archives and Manuscripts: A Select Bibliography**, N.p.: Society of American Archivists, 1975, p. 115-118. This unannotated bibliography of books and articles is organized under these headings: basic reading; development, procedures and problems; select reference works; institutional programs and holdings; and bibliographic aids.

4 Fox, John J. "Bibliography Up-date." **Oral History Review** (1977), 48-57. This bibliography lists books, articles, manuals, catalogs and guides, student publications and journals (published since Waserman's 1975 revision).

5 _____. "Window on the Past: A Guide to Oral History." **Choice** 17 (June 1980), 495-508. Guides, manuals and catalogs in periodical and monographic form are cited by Fox in this bibliographic essay. Though some items stray into the area of cultural journalism, this is probably the largest bibliography on oral history in terms of number of citations.

6 Gibson, Michael D. "A Selective Bibliography of Oral History." **Annals of Iowa** 44 (Spring 1979), 654-657. Gibson selected those books and articles on the how-to-do-it aspect of oral history. He lists journals which are devoted solely to oral history or which consistently publish articles on the subject.

7 Grainger, Bruce. "Information Sources for Oral History in Canada." **Ontario Library Review** 65 (June 1981), 124-128. Canadian oral history associations, periodicals, manuals, union lists and selected books based on oral history are listed.

8 Grele, Ronald J. **Oral History: An Annotated Bibliography.** N.p.: ERIC Clearinghouse on Reading and Communication Skills, 1975. (Readers Advisory Service, Selected Topical Booklists No. 370). The books and articles Grele selected are for the novice and contain basic information. Books incorporating oral history material are listed in a separate section.

9 Hand, Samuel B. "Some Words on Oral Histories." **Scholarly Publishing** 9 (January 1978), 171-185. In this gracefully written bibliographic essay Hand incorporates a history of the movement, chiefly in the U.S.

10 Kusnerz, Peggy Ann. "Oral History: A Selective Bibliography." **Drexel Library Quarterly** 15 (October 1979), 50-75. The bibliographies of Fox and Waserman are updated by Kusnerz in this well planned article. The chief headings are: manuals and handbooks; interviewing techniques; theory; as a teaching device; libraries and archives; international perspectives; research; the profession; periodicals. There are some annotations.

11 Morrissey, Charles T. "Oral History: More Than Tapes Are Spinning." **Library Journal** 105 (April 15, 1980), 932-933. Ordering information for the state and area guides listed is included.

12 Schippers, Donald J., and Adelaide Tusler. **A Bibliography of Oral History.** Los Angeles, Calif.: Oral History Association, 1968. Aimed at the professional, this annotated bibliography lists material published to June, 1968. It excludes articles on how to use tape recorders and AV equipment and printed interviews.

13 Stansell, Jan. "Oral History: A Selected List of Resources." **Collection Building** 2, #3 (1980), 52-63. Topics included in this annotated bibliography are: general and historical works; methodological considerations; manuals; lists and directories; bibliographies; works incorporating oral history material; oral history outside the U.S.; legal aspects; libraries and oral history; oral history in education; and oral history applied to other disciplines.

14 Stenberg, Henry G. "Selected Bibliography, 1977-81." **Oral History Review** 10 (1982), 119-132. Stenberg cites works on "the theory and practice of oral history and/or employment of oral history collections or interviews in a major way."

15 Waserman, Manfred J. **Bibliography on Oral History,**
rev. ed. New York: Oral History Association, 1975.
This three part bibliography of just under 400 citations
lists items which appeared up to early 1975: 1) books
and articles on oral history; 2) catalogs of outstanding
collections; 3) recent books based on oral history interviews. Subject index.

Books and Articles on Oral History

16 Adamovich, Ales. "With the People As a Co-author."
Soviet Literature 5 (1979), 109-114. Stories of the
Leningrad blockade of World War II gathered by the
author from Russian survivors.
17 "Ageism Attacked Through Oral History Project." **Aging**
#289, (November/December, 1978), 45. A short account
of a project of the Maine Committee on Aging seeking
new directions for policy development.
18 Agiri, Babatunde. "Oral Traditions and the Study of the
U.S. and Africa." **American Studies International** 17,
(Winter, 1979), 67-71. The author uses the oral traditions
of Africa to support the legitimacy of oral history
data. He feels African sources were slighted by white
historians who relied solely on written records. To
the detriment of history, the reverse situation is becoming the norm with Americans using oral history and
African historians not giving it enough weight.
19 Alban, J.R. "Tape-recording Local History in Swansea."
Local Historian [Great Britain] 14, #5 (1981), 284-288.
An account of a project in Swansea from its inception
to the handling of the finished tapes.
20 Albert F. Simpson Historical Research Center. **USAF
Oral History Catalog.** Washington, D.C.: Office of
Air Force History, 1977.
21 Alice Lloyd College, Appalachian State University, Emory
and Henry College, Lees Junior College. **The Appalachian
Oral History Project Union Catalog.** 1977. The project's
focus is the collection of the history and folklore of
Central Appalachia. A comprehensive subject index
covers material annotated by the four co-operating
schools. Major and minor topics of each interview
and the sound quality of the tape are included in the
annotation.
22 Allen, Barbara. "Personal Point of View in Orally Communicated History." **Western Folklore** 38 (April 1979),

110-118. Allen explores the distrust traditional historians have of oral tradition pointing out that oral history is meant to supplement not supplant written sources. She relates oral history to folklore because both are based on personal perceptions.

23 _____. "Talking About the Past: A Folkloristic Study of Orally Communicated History." Doctoral Dissertation, University of California at Los Angeles, 1980. (Dissertation Abstracts, 41:1710A). A study of the point of view of the interviewee vis a vis the interviewer and an analysis of the context in which the material was recorded. Two months fieldwork in Silver Lake, Oregon, was the basis for the study.

24 _____, and William Lynwood Montell. **From Memory to History: Using Oral Sources in Local Historical Research.** Nashville, Tenn.: American Association for State and Local History, 1981. The authors intend this handbook "for researchers...reconstructing and writing local history." Five chapters deal with the interviewer's role, differences between oral and written history and ways to test for validity. The final chapter has ideas for using oral material in printed form. The text is lucidly presented and could be used by high school students. Appendices demonstrate through examples points made in the text. Bibliography of works cited.

Allen, Charles, see **Tales From a Dark Continent.**

25 Allen, Richard B. "New Orleans Jazz Archive at Tulane." **Wilson Library Bulletin** 40 (March, 1966), 619-623. The archive began in 1958 and collects interviews with jazz greats and non-musicians. Tapes are never erased because the project directors are convinced that no transcription is ever perfect. Tapes with jazz buffs throughout the U.S. and abroad, phonorecords, sheet music and photographs are also preserved.

26 Allen, Rodney F., and John R. Meyer. "Beyond Collecting Information: Oral History as Social Education." **History and Social Science Teacher** 15 (Winter, 1980), 101-108. The authors urge classroom teachers to not only collect data but to use the material for the socialization of adolescents. They believe that students are affected by what they hear and identify with the speakers. Extensive bibliography.

27 Allen, Susan Emily. "Resisting the Editorial Ego: Editing Oral History." **Oral History Review** 10 (1982), 33-45. Allen asserts "editing oral history is...nothing more

and nothing less than facilitating access on paper to the materials on tape" and urges a "uniform standard of excellence."

28 American Indian Research Project. **Oyate Iyechunka Woglakapi: The People Speak for Themselves; An Oral History Collection.** Vermillion, S.D.: 1970- . These volumes are a catalog of spoken interviews and music. Non-Indians and the Plains Indians with whom they worked are both listed. Subjects covered include mythology, folklore and customs, art and music. Interviewer, place and date are recorded. Listings are by interviewee and location.

29 Ames, Lynn. "About Westchester." **New York Times,** February 22, 1981, Section 22, p. 2. The Westchester County Oral History Project is concerned with the ethnic heritage of the area's population. The county historical society is training volunteers to conduct interviews as part of its Tricentennial in 1983.

Anderson, R. Wayne, see #1.

Andresen, Carl Erik, see Burchardt, Jorgan.

30 Anthony, Arthe Agnes. "The Negro Creole Community in New Orleans, 1880-1920: An Oral History." Doctoral dissertation, University of California, Irvine, 1978. (Dissertation Abstracts, 39:5666A). The group maintained its cohesiveness by virtue of its language, social and cultural heritage. Little mention is made of the methodology of interviewing. Similarities and contrasts with other black communities point up the uniqueness of this one.

31 Appel, Benjamin. **The People Talk: American Voices From the Great Depression.** Reprint of 1940 ed. New York: Simon and Schuster, 1982. In 1939 and 1940 Appel traveled across the country recording what people had to say about life in America. He went from coast to coast, from New York City to a lumber camp. There is no description of his methodology. Though not intended as "oral history" it makes an interesting comparison with Terkel's **Hard Times.**

32 Arceneaux, Tom E. "Learning and Lagniappe in Louisiana." **Childhood Education** 54 (March, 1978), 238-241. The author, a teacher in Louisiana, describes some efforts at cultural journalism in the Foxfire mode. Short bibliography.

33 "The Archives of American Art Oral History Program: A Preliminary Guide to the Tape-recorded Interviews." **Archives of American Art Journal** 8 (January, 1968),

1-21; 9 (January, 1969), 1-20. Begun in 1959 the Archives include (c. 1968) 300 interviews, 128 of which have been transcribed. A list of 78 transcripts are reprinted here by name of interviewee with a brief description of the material covered. Pages 9-21 contain the transcript of an interview with Hudson Walker concerning American painter Marsden Hartley. In the January, 1969 issue 65 more transcripts are described. Pages 10-16 are a transcript of an interview with Abraham Walkowitz.

34 Armitage, Susan. "Housework and Childrearing on the Frontier: The Oral History Record." **Sociology and Social Research** 63 (April, 1979), 467-474. Twenty Colorado women were interviewed on the subject of housework and childrearing in the 1920's. Their average age at the time of the interview was 85. They lived on mountain ranches or in mining camps or homesteaded. They discuss methods of cleaning, washing and cooking. A primary goal was the expenditure of as little cash as possible, making barter common. Childrearing was done in between the rest of the chores.

35 Ashbrook, James B., tr. and ed. "Paul Tillich in Conversation: Culture and Religion." **Foundations** 14 (January-March 1971), 6-17;14 (April-June 1971), 102-115;14 (July-September 1971), 209-223. Tillich and Ashbrook discuss several topics: Protestantism, Catholicism and art; conservative and liberal Protestant theology; and Christianity and other world religions.

36 Ashdown, Ellen. "Florida's Black Archives: A Substantial Past." **Change** 11 (April, 1979), 48-49. The Black Archives Research Center and Museum at Tallahassee's Florida A and M University is a depository for taped interviews with black and white southerners 65 years old and over. Director James Eaton describes the collection and some of the changes brought about by desegregation.

37 Aural History Convention, University of British Columbia, 1973. **Proceedings: Aural History Convention.** J. Covernton, and W.J. Langlois, eds. Vancouver: Reynoldston Research and Studies, 1973.

38 Austin, Judith. "New Horizons in Oral History: The Ninth Annual Colloquium of the Oral History Association." **Oral History Review** (1975), 82-94. A summary of the talks and discussions at the Ninth Colloquium.

39 Avery, Laurence G. "Maxwell Anderson's Report on Frank Cobb's Interview with Woodrow Wilson: The Documentary

Source." **North Dakota Quarterly** 45 (Summer, 1977),
5-14. The dispute over the date of this interview and
whether it really took place or was a fabrication put
together by Anderson and Laurence Stallings is discussed.
A transcript complete with crossed out words is reproduced. Sixteen notes.

Baca, Beverly, see Jensen, Joan.

40 Bailey, David Thomas. "Divided Prism: Two Sources
of Black Testimony on Slavery." **Journal of Southern
History** 46 (August, 1980), 381-404. Forty autobiographies of blacks and 637 WPA Writers' Projects interviews
are the basis of the author's comparative analysis.
Blacks interviewed were older at the time of the interview than were those who wrote autobiographies. Diet,
religion, general treatment, and family life are covered.
Slaves who wrote autobiographies lived under slavery
more years of their lives than did interviewees. Bailey
concludes the two sources disagree on major points
in their descriptions of the lives of slaves.

41 Bailinson, Frank. "Recollections of Nixon as a Youth
to Appear in Print." **New York Times,** March 3, 1978,
p. 15. The California State University campus at Fullerton gathered 179 oral histories of Nixon. Interviews
conducted from 1969 to 1971 will be published in microfilm and fiche by Microfilming Corporation of America.
Coverage extends from Nixon's boyhood through his
college years.

42 Bainer, Roy. **The Engineering of Abundance: An Oral
History Memoir.** Davis: Oral History Center, University
of California, 1975. An interview with Roy Bainer
about agricultural engineering. Reviewed in **California
Historical Quarterly** 55 (Spring 1976), 85-86.

43 Baldwin, B.S. "Public Library of South Australia's Oral
History Project, 1903-1908." **Archives and Manuscripts**
6 (August 1976), 292-302.

44 Ballew, Stephen. **"Suthin" (It's the Opposite of Nothin'):
An Oral History of Grover Morrison's Woods Operation
at Little Musquash Lake, 1945-1947.** Orono, Me.:
Northeast Folklore Society, 1978. Concerns the Maine
lumber industry. Reviewed: **Journal of American Folklore**
94 (July-September 1981), 387-388; **Journal of Forest
History** 24 (April 1980), 101-102.

Banks, Ann, see **First Person America.**

45 Banks, Lynne Reid. **Torn Country: An Oral History of
the Israeli War of Independence.** New York: Watts,
1982. The 1947-49 Arab-Israeli war is the subject of

this oral history. Most of the 60 plus interviews were conducted in English. Excerpts are arranged by topic (desert campaigns, the role of women, etc.) so that the words of each of the interviewees are scattered throughout the book. Brief biographical notes, index, maps.

46 Barnard, Roy S. **Oral History.** Carlisle Barracks, Pa.: U.S. Army Military History Research Collection, 1976. (Special Bibliographic Series 13). (D 114.14:13/v. 1 and 2). Barnard lists transcripts from the Senior Officer Oral History Program. There is detailed information on each man's military service record. Interviewers are named and the place and date of the taping are noted. Cross reference index to topics.

47 Barnett, C. Robert. "Use of Oral History and Interviews as Research Techniques in Sport History." **Physical Educator** 39 (December 1982), 187-189. Barnett emphasizes preliminary research before the interview and verification of the date obtained as important requisites of a successful project. He includes examples and a short bibliography.

48 Barnhart, Jacqueline B. "Doing Oral History: The Yountville Project." **AHA Newsletter** 18 (December 1980), 5-7. An account of the author's project with veterans hospitalized in Yountville, California. Biographical material on the men was recorded by the author and her students. She observed that the 'chemistry' between interviewer and the subject often determined the quality of the product. Few of the vets were career military men leading Barnhart to concentrate on their individual experiences.

49 Bartlett, Richard A. "Some Thoughts After the 3rd National Colloquium on Oral History." **Journal of Library History** 4 (April 1969), 169-72. A view of the colloquium by a traditional historian who believes librarians should be running oral history programs. "Oral history **per se** is a collector's and a custodian's job, not a[n] historian's."

50 Baskin, John. **New Burlington: The Life and Death of an American Village.** New York: Norton, 1976. The author interviewed the people of an Ohio town before it was obliterated by a reservoir. He provides connecting material, photos and excerpts from diaries and letters.

51 Bates, J. Leonard. "The 'Kingfish' Seen Through Oral History." **Historian** 34 (November 1971), 116-120. A review of **Huey Long** the biography by T. Harry Williams

in which he made extensive use of oral history interviews.

52 Bauer, Elizabeth. "Prytanean Oral History." **Journal of Library History** 6 (April 1971), 163-168. Bauer reports on a program recording the history of the Prytanean Society at Berkeley, California, the oldest scholastic-activities honor society for women in the U.S.

53 Baum, Willa K. "Building Community Identity Through Oral History: A New Role for the Local Library." **California Librarian** 31 (October 1970), 271-284. Baum believes libraries are the best depositories of local history listing continuity and preservation as primary reasons. She describes the equipment needed, gives rules for interviewing and handling of the material produced. Some current California projects are cited.

54 _____. "History on Tape: The Regional Oral History Office at the Bancroft Library." **California Historical Quarterly** 54 (Spring 1975), 77-79. An account of the inception, funding and holdings of an archive at Berkeley.

55 _____. "The Library as Guardian of Oral History Materials: An Example from Berkeley." **Catholic Library World** 47 (October 1975), 112-117. A description of how oral history material is handled by the Bancroft Library: preservation, cataloging, notation of restrictions and use by patrons are some of the topics Baum covers. Catalog cards and a release form are reproduced in the text. Bibliography.

56 _____. "Oral History: A Revived Tradition at the Bancroft Library." **Pacific Northwest Quarterly** 58 (April 1967), 57-64. The director of the library's Regional Oral History Office links the present movement to the work conducted by Hubert Howe Bancroft in the late nineteenth century. She outlines the early days of the twentieth century project and cites examples of current work.

57 _____. "Oral History and the Historical Society." **California Historian** 14 (1967), 143-146. Baum summarizes a meeting of the Conference of the California Historical Societies devoted to making and using tapes to promote history.

58 _____. **Oral History for the Local Historical Society.** 2nd ed. Nashville, Tenn.: American Association for State and Local History, 1975. A landmark publication in the field and an excellent starting text for the beginner. Baum's 19 tips for interviewers will be forever relevant.

59 _____. "Oral History in the West." **California Librarian** 3 (January 1972), 29-37. Among the projects described are: the University of California's Bancroft Library, UCLA, Claremont Graduate School, Doris Duke Indian Oral History Project, Forest History Society and others in the Trans-Mississippi West.

60 _____. "Oral History, the Library and the Genealogical Researcher." **Journal of Library History** 5 (October 1970), 359-371. Baum discusses the value of oral history for the genealogist and explores ways it can be used to obtain genealogical information. Transcriptions which form the nucleus of the Bancroft Library's collection are consulted by researcher's tracking ancestors who went west. Some of the library's projects are listed with examples: general, regional and special subjects; ethnic and cultural communities; outstanding people of achievement; institutional history. Baum makes a plea that oral historians ask their interviewees for information on family background and ancestors.

61 _____. "Therapeutic Value of Oral History." **International Journal of Aging and Human Development** 12, #1 (1980/ 1981), 49-53. Author believes the therapeutic value of oral history to the interviewer grows out of a program of rigorous historical value.

62 _____. **Transcribing and Editing Oral History.** Nashville, Tenn.: American Association for State and Local History, 1977. A guide for anyone involved with processing oral history material, this slim book is laid out in very practical terms. Baum takes for granted most projects are underfunded and suggests more than one method for almost every contingency. Transcription, editing and indexing are covered in detail. Sample pages are reprinted and a 33 1/3 rpm sound recording is included. Annotated bibliography.

63 _____, and Amelia Fry. **Oral History Program Manual.** New York: Praeger, 1974. Reviewed: **American Archivist** 37 (October 1974), 583-586.

_____, see also California. University. Regional Oral History Office; Fry, Amelia R.

64 Beasley, Maurine, and Richard R. Harlow. "Oral History: Additional Research Tool for Journalism Historians." **Journalism History** 7 (Spring 1980), 38-39. A brief description of what oral history is with a list of do's and don't's for interviewers.

65 Beilman, James. "The University of Iowa Oral History Project." **Books at Iowa** #27 (November 1977), 21-29.

The Iowa project is devoted to chronicling the development and growth of the university. Beilman lists fourteen topics and incidents which appear in the collection. Among them: building projects and remodelings; founding of new departments; athletics; and the effect of national events on the university. Name of participants and the subject of their interviews are listed.

66 Benison, Saul. "Oral History and Manuscript Collecting." Isis 53 (March 1962), 113-117. Oral history can provide historical material in situations where written records have been lost, destroyed or never made at all. Benison emphasizes thorough preparation before the interview and outlines a program for the training of oral historians.

67 _____. "Reflections on Oral History." American Archivist 28 (January 1965), 71-77. The author believes that autobiography as done by the oral historian is "àn attempt at a first interpretation of a series of given events." He urges the inclusion of the interviewer's questions and a bibliography of sources in the final transcript. Methods for using oral history in the educational process are suggested.

68 _____. "Rene Dubos and the Capsular Polysaccharide of Pneumococcus: An Oral History Memoir." Bulletin of the History of Medicine 50, #4 (1976), 459-477. An excerpt of an interview conducted by Benison is printed here by special permission. The entire interview is closed until five years after Dubos' death. His early work at the Rockefeller Institute and his ground-breaking research in immunology are dealt with in this extract.

69 _____. Tom Rivers: Reflections on a Life in Medicine and Science. Cambridge, Mass.: M.I.T. Press, 1967. Benison interviewed virus research Dr. Thomas Rivers about his education and medical career; the organizations he worked within; and the problems of scientific research. Questions and answers are transcribed. There is little information on Rivers' family or personal life because he put those subjects off limits.

70 Bennett, Clifford T. "Black Roots; Using Genealogy in the Classroom." Social Studies 71 (March/April 1980), 68-70. This brief article suggests oral interviews with black students' families as a way to supplement written records.

71 Bennett, James. Oral History and Delinquency: The Rhetoric of Criminology. Chicago: University of Chicago Press, 1981. Bennett investigates the use of life histories to understand young criminals. He examines the condi-

tions that brought about the recording of these histories, especially Henry Mayhew's work in nineteenth century London. The University of Chicago sociology department used life histories to develop hypotheses about delinquents and their behavior.

72 Benson, Ezra Taft. "Oral History: Ezra Taft Benson." **Idaho Heritage** #10 (1977), 12-15. Benson, who was Secretary of Agriculture under Eisenhower from 1953 to 1961, talks about his Mormon heritage and his work in government.

Berk, Stephen M. see Brown, Lucille W.

73 Berman, Leo H. "Oral History as Source Material for the History of Behavioral Sciences." **Journal of the History of the Behavioral Sciences** 3 (January 1967), 58-59. Berman presses for the use of oral history to preserve people's recollections and cites several current programs.

74 Bertaux, Daniel. "The Bakers of France." **History Today** 33 (June 1983), 33-37. Sociologist Bertaux chronicles his foray into oral history for an investigation of the lives of French bakers. He interviewed apprentices, bakers and their wives and retails several examples of his findings. He advocates talking with a variety of individuals before drawing conclusions.

75 Bilstein, Roger E. "The Oral History Collection at Columbia University." **Aerospace Historian** 22 (Spring 1975), 46-47. The author lists holdings of the Columbia collection which have relevance to aeronautics and astronautics. The Air Force Academy Project, Marine Corps Project and Naval History Project are briefly described.

76 **Black Elk Speaks: Being the Life Story of a Holy Man of the Oglala Sioux as Told Through John G. Neihardt.** Reprint of 1932 ed. with a new preface. Lincoln: University of Nebraska Press, 1961. Neihardt, an accomplished poet, met Black Elk in the course of researching and writing a long narrative poem. This book is the result of meetings conducted in May, 1931. Because Black Elk spoke no English his son interpreted and Neihardt's daughter acted as stenographer. An appendix compares a portion of Neihardt's transcript with the stenographic draft. Photos and drawings.

77 Blinman, Eric, Elizabeth Colson, and Robert F. Heizer. "A Makah Epic Journey: Oral History and Documentary Sources." **Pacific Northwest Quarterly** 68, #4 (1977), 153-163. In the early nineteenth century four Makah men were kidnapped from the coast of present-day

Washington State and taken by ship to California. Colson recorded the incident in 1941-42 in interviews with Makah people. Three transcripts are reproduced at the end of the article. Documentary evidence is cited.

78 Blois, B.A. "Humanizing History." **Community College Review** 4 (February 1976), 15-17. Blois believes many college history survey courses are too broad in the range of topics covered. He urges instructors to introduce an oral history project to stimulate student interest. His example is that old standby, the Great Depression.

79 Blythe, Ronald. **Akenfield: Portrait of an English Village.** London: Pantheon Books, 1969. Blythe interviewed people in Suffolk in 1967 about their lives and their village. An introduction recounts the history of the place and its isolation from the life of the surrounding area. Orchards took over land once devoted to cereal crops and the population shift from rural locale to city is discussed. Farmers, a blacksmith, the veterinarian and a gravedigger are among those interviewed. Short bibliography on English village life.

80 _____. **The View in Winter: Reflections on Old Age.** New York: Harcourt Brace Jovanovich, 1979. The aged of England are Blythe's subjects. The village is unidentified as are speakers beyond age and occupation. Edited down to beautiful, flowing prose, the volume has been criticized for that very reason.

81 Bobowski, Rita. "Living History." **Space World** (May 1982), 25, 35. A short, popular account of the American Institute of Physics Oral History Project.

Bolin, Barbara see Jensen, Joan.

82 Bonfield, Lynn A. "Conversation with Arthur M. Schlesinger, Jr.: The Use of Oral History." **American Archivist** 43 (Fall 1980), 461-472. A transcript of Bonfield's talk with Schlesinger concerning his use of oral history techniques for books about the Kennedys. Topics include his own research and that of contemporaries Dean Acheson, Theodore H. White.

83 Bonomo, Josephine. "Making History by Talking." **New York Times,** April 21, 1974, p. 78. A report on the Newark Public Library project aimed at filling in gaps in the local history collection.

84 Borchuck, Fred Paul. Executive Succession in Academic Libraries: An Examination of Succession Using Oral History." Doctoral dissertation, Rutgers University,

1978. (Dissertation Abstracts 39:3895A). The author tested hypotheses found in administrative succession research literature by conducting 13 oral history interviews of those appointed to university library directorships from 1971 to 1973. A major part of the dissertation discusses the findings of the study. The use of oral history in succession research is weighed.

Bornat, Joanna, see #2.

85 Bornet, Vaughn Davis. "Oral History Can Be Worthwhile." **American Archivist** 18, #3 (1955), 241-253. Interviewing became an accepted form of journalism in the 1860's. Bornet gives a brief overview of the technique to the early 1950's. He lists 14 minimum standards, among them: transcripts should identify the interviewer and note time and place; the interviewer should describe the tone and manner of the subject; both questions and answers appear in the transcript, use of legal release forms.

86 Botkin, B.A., ed. **Lay My Burden Down: A Folk History of Slavery.** Chicago: University of Chicago Press, 1945. This compilation of excerpts from interviews with former slaves was a WPA Writers' Project. Material was gathered from 1936 to 1938 and is arranged by theme: tall tales, "hants," anecdotes, the Civil War and its aftermath. Speakers are briefly identified in an appendix and interviewers named. Index.

87 Boyd, Lois A., and R. Douglas Brackenridge. "Oral History: An Introduction." **Journal of Presbyterian History** 56 (Spring 1978), 3-9. The authors give an overview of oral history and discuss an ongoing project of the Presbyterian Historical Society. An interview release form sample is reproduced. Transcripts of interviews with five people including the first woman ordained a Presbyterian minister are reprinted on pages 10-78. A brief biographical sketch is provided along with the name of the interviewer.

Brackenridge, R. Douglas see Boyd, Lois A.

88 Bragg, Melvyn. **Speak for England: An Oral History of England, 1900-1975, Based on Interviews with Inhabitants of Wigton, Cumberland.** New York: Knopf, 1977. Bragg interviewed people aged eight to 80 from all walks of life in his home town of Wigton. Chapters covering specific events or time periods alternate with the testimony of a single speaker on a variety of topics. In a postscript the author offers some observations about changes in English life since the beginning of

the century. Those interviewed are named and briefly described, a practice which makes them more "alive" and real for the reader. (Compare Broadfoot's works.) Appendices expand the description of individuals quoted in the body of the book and the town of Wigton.

89 Bravo, Anna. "Solidarity and Loneliness: Piedmontese Peasant Women at the Turn of the Century." **International Journal of Oral History** 3 (June 1982), 76-91. Bravo reports on her study of 40 married women and the impact of rites of passage on their lives.

90 Brigham Young University. Historical Dept. **Guide to the James Moyle Oral History Program.** Salt Lake City: History Dept., Church of Jesus Christ of Latter-Day Saints, 1977.

91 Broadfoot, Barry. **The Pioneer Years 1895-1914: Memories of Settlers Who Opened the West.** New York: Doubleday, 1976. Broadfoot covers the years when the Canadian West was opened by pioneering homesteaders who had the dollars for a filing fee. Those who didn't found other ways to make a living. He gathered their recollections with tape recorder and pen and arranged them by topic.

92 _____. **Six War Years 1939-1945: Memories of Canadians at Home and Abroad.** New York: Doubleday, 1974. From the vantage of the 1970's, Canadians look back on their lives in the second world war. As in his other books, Broadfoot does not identify the speakers. Some of the topics: enlistment and training; women in uniform; building the Alaska Highway; and buddies. The animosity between the English and French over the Zombies, conscripted Canadians who were promised they would never be sent overseas, is remembered by many today.

93 _____. **Ten Lost Years, 1919-1929: Memories of Canadians Who Survived the Depression.** Toronto, Doubleday Canada, 1973. In this Canadian version of Terkel's **Hard Times** Broadfoot groups his material by subject without identifying the speaker. Some speeches were tape recorded, others written up from memory or notes. Photos.

94 _____. **Years of Sorrow, Years of Shame: The Story of Japanese Canadians in World War II.** New York: Doubleday, 1977. The experiences of Canadians of Japanese ancestery during the relocations of the 1940's were recorded by Broadfoot. Many were born in Canada and others were naturalized before the war began. The material is thematically arranged and Broadfoot provides a short introduction for each topic. Photos.

95 Brodman, Estelle. "Education and Attitudes of Early Medical Librarians to Their Work: A Discussion Based on the Oral History Project of the Medical Library Association." **Journal of Library History** 15 (Spring 1980), 167-182. Three medical librarians, Mary Louise Marshall, Janet Doe, and Bertha B. Hallam, discuss why they entered the profession. Their training, their era (before and after World War I), and individual accomplishments are covered in the interview transcripts.

96 _____. "Possible Uses of MLA's Oral History Taped Interviews." **Medical Library Association Bulletin** 69 (January 1981), 34-36. Describes material collected and suggests some projects.

97 Brown, Courtney. "Oral History and the Oral Tradition of Black America: The Kinte Foundation." **Oral History Review** (1973), 26-28. The transcription of a speech given in 1973 explaining the work of the foundation. The focus is on oral history research conducted on the Eastern seaboard.

98 Brown, James Seay, Jr., ed. **Up Before Daylight: Life Histories from the Alabama Writers' Project, 1938-1939.** University: University of Alabama Press, 1982. These 28 life histories were gathered by the listeners without benefit of tape recorders. The introduction (with 64 footnotes) provides background on the project's development under the direction of William T. Couch. The accounts are grouped by geographic area. Both interviewer and subject are named and each history is preceded by explanatory remarks. An appendix describes 56 unpublished Alabama life histories. Bibliography, index, photos.

99 Brown, Lucille W., and Stephen M. Berk. "Fathers and Sons: Hasidim, Orthodoxy, and Haskalah—A View From Eastern Europe." **Oral History Review** (1977), 17-32. Brown and Berk present excerpts from interviews with five East European Jewish men of the **shtetel** on the impact of the Jewish Enlightenment on their lives.

100 Brown, Lyle. "Methods and Approaches in Oral History: Interviewing Latin American Elites." **Oral History Review** (1975), 77-86. The author gives an overview of the work of James W. Wilkie's work with Latin American political leaders. He quotes liberally from Wilkie's research and discusses his own labors in Texas politics. Bibliographical references.

101 Brown, Marley, III. "The Use of Oral and Documentary

Sources in Historical Archaeology: Ethnohistory at the Mott Farm." **Ethnohistory** 20 (Fall 1973), 347-360. The report of a multi-disciplinary investigation into life on a Portsmouth, Rhode Island, farm dating from the early seventeenth century. Oral history research was used to document economic activity and life styles of the twentieth century inhabitants. Archaeologists' searches for locations of specific sites (e.g. privy, cemetery) were facilitated by oral history interviews.

102 Brown, Robert F. **The New New Englanders.** Worcester, Mass.: Commonwealth Press, 1980. Newcomers to Southbridge, Massachusetts, talk about their lives.

103 Bryant, V.J.M. "Talking to Octogenarians: A Key to Their Memories." **Local Historian** 10 (November 1972), 183-185. Bryant has found that showing public records to his subjects often jogs their memories, bringing up a wealth of information and unraveling problems for him. He believes short visits on a regular basis are more fruitful than marathon sessions with the elderly.

104 Buckendorf, Madeline. "The Idaho Oral History Center: New Resources for Libraries." **Idaho Librarian** 34 (April 1982), 54-58. A program run by the Idaho State Historical Society is outlined. Workshops, a cataloging project and available publications are listed with addresses for further information.

105 _____, and Margot H. Knight. "Oral History and Historic Preservation: A Case Study in Washington and Idaho." **Oral History Review** 9 (1981), 97-114. Both states use oral history techniques and the team approach in survey registration of sites in different ways. Two sample cities and the practices of other states are discussed.

106 Bullock, Paul, ed. **Watts: The Aftermath, an Inside View of the Ghetto, by the People of Watts.** New York: Grove, 1969. A view of Watts as seen by its residents. The editor began his work a year before the August, 1965, riot and continued almost to the time of publication. Chapters are thematically arranged; schools, welfare, etc. The situation before, during and after the riot are covered in opening chapters. Biographical material, glossary.

107 Bundy, Colin, and Dermot Healy. "Aspects of Urban Poverty." **Oral History** 6 (Spring 1978), 79-97. The authors quote from interviews conducted for several

different projects illustrating how peoples' lives were colored by poverty.

108 Burchardt, Jorgan, and Carl Erik Andresen. "Oral History, People's History and Social Change in Scandinavia." **Oral History** 8, #2 (1980), 25-29. Folklorists, historians, sociologists and ethnologists have all collected Scandinavian history using oral methods in the past. Life histories, study circles and workers doing factory history are some of today's forms.

Burchardt, Natasha, see Thompson, Paul.

109 Burg, Maclyn P. "An Oral Historian in Moscow: Some Firsthand Observations." **Oral History Review** (1974), 10-23. Burg gives an account of his experiences and frustrations in trying to interview Russian army officers about the last days of World War II.

110 Bury, John C. **The Historical Role of Arizona's Superintendent of Public Instruction.** N.p.: 1974. ED 114 975. For the period from 1854 to 1958 Bury writes a straight narrative history of the superintendents of public instruction and their impact on public education in the state. He conducted oral history interviews with ex-superintendents and their co-workers to chronicle the period from 1958 to 1975.

Busha, Charles H., see McCombs, Carol.

111 Butler, Robert N., M.D. "Life Review: An Unrecognized Bonanza." **International Journal of Aging and Human Development** 12, #1 (1980/1981), 35-38. The author uses oral history techniques in treating patients and advocates its use as therapy.

112 Byington, Robert, et al. "Collecting Oral History." In **Kin and Communities: Families in America,** Allan J. Lichtman and Joan R. Challinor, eds. (Washington, D.C.: Smithsonian Institution, 1979), p.265-284. This is the transcript of a panel discussion. Participants in the Folklife Program of the Smithsonian talk about their experiences and methods of gathering material.

113 Cadle, Dean, and Richard Reed. "Thomas Wolfe at 75." **Appalachian Heritage** 3 (Summer 1975), 45-58. American novelist Thomas Wolfe was born in 1900 and died in 1938. The authors look back on his life and work with hindsight from the vantage of what would have been his 75th birthday.

114 California. University. Berkeley. Bancroft Library. **Interviews Completed or in Process.** Berkeley: 1966.

115 _____, _____. Regional Oral History Office. **Catalogue of the Regional Oral History Office, 1954-1979.**

Suzanne B. Riess, and Willa K. Baum, eds. Berkeley: University of California, Bancroft Library, 1980. Reviewed: **Journal of Forest History** 24 (October 1980), 205-206.

116 Campbell, D'Ann, and Richard Jensen. "Community and Family History at the Newberry Library: Some Solutions to a National Need." **History Teacher** 11 (November 1977), 47-54. The authors outline a Newberry program conducted in co-operation with the Chicago Historical Society called Workshops in Community History which are designed to help laymen undertake genealogical research. These workshops and a program in state and community history at the college level both utilize oral history.

117 Campbell, Ronald. **Guide to an Oral History Archive for · the City of Santa Clara, California.** Boulder, Col.: Western Interstate Commission for Higher Education, 1974.

118 Cash, Joseph H., and Herbert T. Hoover. **To Be an Indian: An Oral History.** New York: Holt, Rinehart and Winston, 1971. This selection of oral history interviews with Indians of the Northern Plains centers on four themes: spiritual life and folklore, reservation life, the eras of the Depression and World War II, life in the 1950's and '60's. Narrators and interviewers are identified as are the place and time of the interview.

119 Cavallini, Donald Jay. "Oral/Aural History, In and Out of the Classroom." **Social Studies** 70 (May/June 1979), 112-117. Cavallini's pupils tape recorded the sounds of streetcars and horse-drawn wagons moving over cobbled streets as aural projects. There is a lengthy description of a field trip to record sounds of banking at a local branch.

120 _____. "Using Oral History in College and High School: A Model for Studying the Great Depression." Doctoral dissertation, Illinois State University, 1980. (Dissertation Abstracts, 41:2257A). The author believes oral history is more effective with college than high school students but is rewarding for both.

121 Cendagorta, Christine. "Grassroots Learning: Connecting Classroom and Community." **Media and Methods** 17 (September 1980), 50-52. Cendagorta describes her work with gifted junior high students in Reno, Nevada. The 1930's Depression in the area was linked to the 1980 economic situation. Questions were studied by the interviewees before the taping. She makes suggestions for other projects, such as having an aspiring doctor interview a medical professional.

122 Chaison, Gary N. "Applications of Oral History to the History of Labour and Business." **Canadian Oral History Association Journal** 3, #2 (1978), 9-17.

123 Charlton, Thomas L. "Oral History: A Resource for Baptist Studies." **Baptist History and Heritage** 10 (July 1975), 130-137. Charlton urges the use of oral history to supplement the paucity of records on certain aspects of the history of Baptists. He quotes from published transcripts in the Baylor Univ. collection.

124 _____. **Oral History for Texans.** Austin: Texas Historical Commission, 1981. Charlton gives a brief overview of the movement noting Texan examples gathered by the LBJ Library in Austin, NASA in Houston, the Dallas Public Library and Denton's North Texas State University. He has ideas for future projects.

125 _____, J.M. Gaskin, and A. Ronald Tonks. "Implementing an Oral History Program." **Baptist History and Heritage** 10 (July 1975), 138-141. Excerpts from a transcript of a panel discussion. The speakers urge the training of lay people as oral historians.

126 "Civil Rights Protests in Tampa: Oral Memoirs of Conflict and Accommodation." **Tampa Bay History** 1 (Spring-Summer 1979), 37-54.

127 Clare, Leo La. "Oral History in Canada: An Overview." **Oral History Review** (1973), 87-91. Canadian oral history has several distinguishing features: non-academics are responsible for most of the work; the material tends not to be transcribed; non-elite interviews are in the majority; and material exists in English, French and Japanese.

128 Claremont, California. Graduate School and University Center. **Claremont Graduate School Oral History Program: A Bibliography.** Claremont, Calif.: Claremont University Center, 1978.

129 Clark, E. Culpepper, Michael J. Hyde, and Eva M. Mc-Mahan. "Communication in the Oral History Interview: Investigating Problems of Interpreting Oral Data." **International Journal of Oral History** 1 (1980), 28-40. The authors see the interview as an interpretative process facilitated by clear communication.

130 _____, _____, and _____. "Developing Instruction in Oral History: A New Avenue for Speech Communication." **Communication Education** 30 (July 1981), 238-244. The authors address oral history from the point

of view of speech teachers seeking a multi-disciplinary approach. They discuss a two semester course combining oral history and speech communication taught at the University of Alabama. Extensive references.

131 Clements, William M. "Personal Narrative, the Interview Context, and Question Tradition." **Western Folklore** 39 (April 1980), 106-112. The author is a folklorist associated with the Mid-South Center for Oral History. He discusses similarities and differences between what oral historians call life histories and folklorists term personal narratives.

132 Cochrane, Ken, ed. **Towards a New Past: Toil and Trouble; An Oral History of Industrial Unrest in the Estevan-Bienfait Coalfields.** Regina: Dept. of Culture and Youth, Government of Saskatchewan, 1975.

133 Cohen, Ronald, et al. "Oral History in Africa." **African Studies Bulletin** 8 (1965), 10-12.

Coles, Jane Hallowell, see Coles, Robert.

134 Coles, Robert. **Children of Crisis.** Boston: Little, Brown, 1964-1977. V. 1: **Children of Crisis: A Study of Courage and Fear;** V. 2: **Migrants, Sharecroppers, Mountaineers;** V. 3: **The South Goes North;** V. 4: **Eskimos, Chicanos, Indians;** V. 5: **Privileged Ones: The Well-off and Rich in America.** This series began as a study of how children and the adults responsible for them manage their lives in the face of stresses from various sources. Coles opens with the desegregation movement in the South and its effects on blacks and whites. The second volume focuses on the rural population; the third on people he met in the course of preparing the first two volumes. Parents and children who moved permanently or temporarily to the North figure in the third book. Adolescents of three ethnic groups in the western U.S. are dealt with in the fourth volume. Children of the wealthy from across America speak about their concerns and fears in the last publication in the series. Conversations were transcribed from notes.

135 _____, and Jane Hallowell Coles. **Women of Crisis: Lives of Struggle and Hope.** New York: Delacorte, 1978. These interviews with five women were edited from material the Coleses gathered in the course of research for other books. A migrant, an Eskimo, and a Chicano talk about their lives in America in the 1960's and '70's. Recent books on American women are cited in a bibliographic essay.

136 _____, and _____. **Women in Crisis II: Lives of Work and Dreams.** New York: Delacorte, 1980. The life histories of five American women are transcribed: Laura works in advertising; Maisie is a bank teller; Sue is a feminist who was active in the Civil Rights Movement in the South; Maria is a Pueblo Indian; Eileen is a nurse from a working class background.

137 Colman, Gould P. "A Farmer Joins the Dairymen's League: An Interview with Fred Sexauer." **New York History** 48 (October 1967), 370-385. Interview excerpt with a short biographical introduction about Sexauer.

138 _____. "Oral History, an Appeal for More Systematic Procedures." **American Archivist** 28 (January 1965), 79-83. Colman sets down some guidelines for successful oral history interviews: breaks in the recording should be noted; accurate transcripts are a must; rapport between the subject and interviewer must be established.

139 _____. "Oral History at Cornell." **Wilson Library Bulletin** 40 (March 1966), 624-628. The article deals with oral history as a research method and uses the Cornell program, which concentrates on agricultural history, as an example. Colman is the project director. He lists some of the mistakes which resulted from inexperience.

140 _____. "Theoretical Models and Oral History Interviews." **Agricultural History** 49 (July 1967), 255-266. The author takes issue with the conclusions of a report on the pricing policies of the milk industry in New York state in the 1930's. He supports his thesis with evidence taken from interviews with industry notables.

Colson, Elizabeth, see Blinman, Eric.

141 Columbia University. Oral History Research Office. **The Oral History Collection of Columbia University.** Elizabeth B. Mason and Louis M. Starr, eds. 4th ed. New York: Oral History Research Office, 1979. The introductory essay includes a bibliography of books whose authors used the Columbia collection in their research. A guide to using the catalog is printed in a question and answer format. Material from interviews with four thousand people is indexed by name, subject and special project.

142 Columbia University Oral History Collection: An Index to the Memoirs in Part I of the Microform Edition. Sanford, S. Car.: Microfilming Corp. of America, 1979. This is a computerized name and subject index to 70,000 references. Every memoir in Part I of the collection was combed. Reel and fiche numbers direct the user to the proper spot.

143 Conaway, Charles William. "Lyman Copeland Draper, 'Father of American Oral History'." **Journal of Library History** 1 (October 1966), 234-235, 238-241, 269. Conaway traces the development of oral history from Herodotus to Hubert Howe Bancroft to Draper. In his work as a librarian Draper anticipated the work of modern oral historians. His life and methods are sketched.

144 Cook, George L. "The Frontier College History Project." **Canadian Oral History Association Journal** 1 (1975-76), 25-29.

145 Cooper, Lee B. "Oral History, Popular Music, and Les McCann." **Social Studies** 67 (May/June 1976), 115-118. The author laments that oral historians are overlooking popular music as a source of social comment and criticism. He examines the improvised lyrics of jazzman Les McCann and suggests ways to conduct oral histories of other music personalities.

146 Cortinovis, Irene E. "Augmenting Manuscript Collections Through Oral History." **American Archivist** 43 (Summer 1980), 367-369. Citing archives which have long contained manuscript material, the author notes how oral history has added to the understanding of past events.

147 _____. "Documenting an Event with Manuscripts and Oral History: The St. Louis Teachers' Strike, 1973." **Oral History Review** (1974), 59-63. Cortinovis is the director of the University of Missouri-St. Louis Oral History Program. She conducted two types of projects: those dealing with a single event and others centered on a single topic, such as immigration to the U.S.

_____, see also Sullivan, Margaret L.

148 Cosbey, Robert C. "Proposal for a Saskatchewan Oral History Project." In **Conceptual Problems in Contemporary Folklore Study,** Gerald Cashion, ed. (Bloomington, Ind.: Folklore Forum, 1973), p.36-55; Reprinted in **Canadian Oral History Association Journal** 2 (1976-77), 69-81. Cosbey developed his ideas for the Saskatchewan project by examining other projects and corresponding with their directors. From this he evolved guidelines for collecting, funding and using the material gathered. This is a good picture of the nuts and bolts necessary to put a project together.

149 Courtwright, David T., Herman Joseph, and Don C. Des Jarlais. "Memories from the Street: Oral Histories of Elderly Methadone Patients." **Oral History Review** 9 (1981), 47-64. An account of a New York state program investigating the history of narcotic use from the addict's viewpoint. Preliminary findings and the questions used in the interviews are set down.

Covernton, J., see Aural History Convention.

150 Cowley, John. "Shack Bullies and Levee Contractors: Studies in the Oral History of a Black Protest Song Tradition." **JEMF Quarterly** 16, #60 (1980), 182-193. Cowley studied black songs of the 1920's.

151 Cox, Diane. "Spoken Words Trace Path of History." **New York Times.** July 4, 1982, Section 23, p.1. Using the University of Connecticut's Center for Oral History project **Connecticut Workers and Changing Technology, 1930-1980,** as a springboard Cox writes about the center's past and current work.

152 Craton, Michael. "Perceptions of Slavery: A Preliminary Excursion into the Possibilities of Oral History in Rural Jamaica." In **Old Roots in New Lands: Historical and Anthropological Perspectives on Black Experiences in the Americas,** Ann M. Pescatello, ed. (Westport, Conn.: Greenwood, 1977), p.263-283. Craton's essay details the methodology of a series of 50 interviews conducted in 1973 with elderly blacks. The project sought to learn what these people had been told in their youth about conditions of slavery as undergone by their ancestors in Jamaica.

153 Crawford, Charles W. "The Development of Oral History Research in Tennessee." **West Tennessee Historical Society Papers** #29 (1975), 100-108. The author cites Tennessee oral history projects begun in the late 1960's including those at Memphis State University, East Tennessee University, Fisk University and the Memphis Public Library. He suggests new projects on the country music industry in Nashville and on the culture and folklore of the Cumberland Plateau.

154 _____. "Oral History." **History News** 29 (July 1974), 156. A summation of the growth of the oral history movement to 1974 with a brief bibliography.

155 _____. "The Oral History Program" **RQ** 12 (Spring 1973), 286-289. The author, who is director of the Oral History Research Office at Memphis State University, discusses biographical and topical projects. He stresses the basic purpose of the programs, giving as an example one of his current projects.

156 _____. "Oral History: The State of the Profession."
Oral History Review (1974), 1-9. Crawford looks
backward at 25 years of the movement's growth and
expresses a hope for increasing professionalism.
157 Crawford, Fred Roberts. "The Holocaust: A Never-ending
Agony." **Annals of the American Academy of Political
and Social Science** #450 (1980), 250-255.
Interviews with American and Allied soldiers, nurses, and Red
Cross people who worked with concentration camp
survivors at the end of World War II is the author's
project. An inter-disciplinary study, its purpose is
to examine the impact of the experience and make
known the truth of the Holocaust's horror.
Crumpacker, Laurie, see Humez, Jean M.
158 "Current British Work in Oral History: Supplementary
List." **Oral History** 4 (Spring 1976), 19-22; 4 (Autumn
1976), 30-37; 5 (Spring 1977), 44-49; also appears
in subsequent issues. A listing by locale of ongoing
projects with brief descriptions.
159 Curtiss, Richard D., et al. **Guide for Oral History Programs.** Fullerton: California State University, Oral
History Program, 1973. The handbook is divided into
three sections: 1) a bibliography of articles on oral
history covering equipment, instruction, research
and cataloging; 2) forms, guidelines and procedures;
3) a detailed catalog of the programs at the Fullerton
campus.
160 Cutler, William W., III. "Accuracy in Oral History Interviewing." **Historical Methods Newsletter** 3, #3 (1970),
1-7. Cutler points to studies in medicine and psychology
which corroborate the inaccuracy of human memory.
A well-prepared interviewer is insurance against
dishonesty on the subject's part but he must also
be aware of the distortion his own biases cause.
161 _____. "Oral History: Its Nature and Uses for Educational History." **History of Education Quarterly** 11
(Summer 1971), 184-194. An overview of projects
conducted to 1971 and an explanation for the novice.
162 Danielson, Larry. "The Folklorist, the Oral Historian,
and Local History." **Oral History Review** (1980), 62-72.
Danielson distinguishes the separate spheres of the
folklorist and oral historian but contends that they
may combine techniques to study local history.
163 Danker, Donald F., ed. "The Wounded Knee Interviews
of Eli S. Ricker." **Nebraska History** 62 (Summer 1981),
151-243. Ricker interviewed Indians from 1905 to

1926 on their relations with whites and the intermittent warfare they conducted. Excerpts of interviews with Indian survivors of the Wounded Knee Massacre are reproduced along with a list of the dead.

164 Davallini, Don. "Oral/Aural History: In and Out of the Classroom." **Social Studies for Teachers and Administrators** 70 (May-June 1979), 112-117.

165 Davis, Cullom. **Oral History: From Tape to Type.** Chicago: American Library Association, 1977. A how-to guide for beginners covers preliminaries to the interview and its conduct; transcription, editing and polishing; distribution of the finished product. Davis urges practitioners to go beyond collection of material and publicize the finished product. Samples of data sheets, notes, index cards, typescript pages and catalog cards are reproduced. A glossary, style sheet and basic bibliography on oral history are contained in appendices.

166 _____. "Tapeworms and Bookworms—Oral History in the Library." **Catholic Library World** 47 (October 1975), 102-103. Davis urges co-operation between historians gathering oral history material and the librarians who preserve and disseminate the end result.

167 Davis, J.C. "Slovene Laborer and His Experience of Industrialization, 1888-1976." **East European Quarterly** 10 (Spring 1976), 2-20. This narrative is based on the author's interview with his father-in-law. Changes in rural village life and the effects of two world wars on this area of Yugoslavia are chronicled.

Davis, O.L., Jr., see Mehaffy, George L.; also 642a.

De Bonfil, Alicia O., see Meyer, Eugenia.

168 Deekle, Peter V., and Douglas O. Michael. "Local History Preservation and Promotion: A New Role for the Community College." **Community College Frontiers** 6 (Summer 1978), 12-15. The authors describe the Alleghany County, Maryland, Local History Program which includes oral history research. Housed in the local community college, it uses the institution's history and speech departments and the community services staff in its work.

169 Deering, Mary Jo. "Oral History and School Integration Research: A Case Study." **Oral History Review** (1979), 27-41. A school integration-busing episode in suburban Washington, D.C., was the focus of a project conducted by George Washington University.

170 Degh, Linda. **People in the Tobacco Belt: Four Lives.** Ottawa: National Museums of Canada, 1975. (Canadian

Centre for Folk Culture Studies, Paper no. 13). The life histories of four Hungarian immigrants to Canada were recorded by Degh in 1971. Participants worked in a tobacco farming region in Ontario. They are introduced and a short chronology of their lives is listed. Interview questions and answers are included in the transcripts. Each account is analyzed in a short epilogue.

171 Dembart, Lee. "Koch Tapes for Posterity." **New York Times.** March 10, 1979, p.22. New York Mayor Koch tapes an account of his activities each week.

172 DeMuth, Phyllis. "Local Oral History Projects." **Sourdough** 18 (April 1981), 4-5. A report on several current Alaskan projects.

173 DePasquale, Thomas A. "Use of Oral History." In **Research Methods in Librarianship: Historical and Bibliographical Methods in Library Research.** Rolland E. Stevens, ed. (Champaign: University of Illinois. Graduate School of Library Science, 1971), p.51-61. An elementary essay narrates the origins of oral history at Columbia University and the birth of the Oral History Association. The author cites the dearth of documentary evidence on the Cuban missile crisis, using it as a prime example of a situation where oral evidence could add to the historical record.

Des Jarlais, Don C., see Courtwright, David T.

174 Devore, Wynetta. "The Education of Blacks in New Jersey, 1900-1930: An Exploration in Oral History." Doctoral dissertation, Rutgers University, 1980. (Dissertation Abstracts, 46:3933-3934A). Twenty-five black New Jerseyites from the southern part of the state are the subject of this study. They taught or studied at the Manual Training and Industrial School in Bordentown. The interviews provide a valuable addition to the history of education in New Jersey.

DeVorkin, David H., see Weart, Spencer R.

175 Dial, Adolph L., and David K. Eliades. **The Only Land I Know: A History of the Lumbee Indians.** San Francisco, Calif.: Indian Historian Press, 1975. ED 101 876. Much of the material in this history of a North Carolina tribe has been obtained through oral history.

176 Dick, Ernest J. "Selection and Preservation of Oral History Interviews." **Drexel Library Quarterly** 15 (October 1979), 35-38. Dick urges the complete identification of interviewer and interviewee with a notation of place and date. Editing should be documented

with deletions indicated. He also describes storage conditions for tapes.

Dirksen, Carolyn, see **An Oral History of Northwestern Colorado.**

177 Dixon, Elizabeth I. "Implications of Oral History in Library History." **Journal of Library History** 1 (January 1966), 59-62, 74. Dixon believes that gaps in written sources can be filled by oral history. She makes a plea for librarians to become involved in oral history programs, especially at the local level. As the library becomes a focus of community history, the public will be more inclined to increase its monetary support.

178 _____. "Oral History: A New Horizon." **Library Journal** 87 (April 1, 1962), 1363-1365. The author was the first oral history librarian in the U.S. Her topic here is the interview itself. She doesn't believe the original tapes should be preserved but urges more careful editing of the transcripts.

179 _____. **The Oral History Program at U.C.L.A.: A Bibliography.** Los Angeles: University of California Library, 1966. The 103 item bibliography of the UCLA collection is arranged alphabetically by speaker. Birth and death dates, a short biographical note on the interviewee's life and career and a few words about the matter of the interview are included. Subject index.

180 Docker, Ted, and Rolf Gerritsen. "The 1934 Kalgoorlie Riots." **Labour History** [Australia] #31 (1976), 79-82. Docker describes his role in the riots. Gerritsen treats them as a historical event and comments on the use of oral evidence.

181 Dolci, Danilo. **Sicilian Lives.** Justin Vitichio, trans. New York: Pantheon Books, 1981. Dolci went to Sicily • in 1952 to work with the poor. The 39 interviews were taken down by him over a period of several years. A few lines introduce each speaker. Sorcery, a Catholic cardinal's soliloquy, healers, and a princess's life story are woven into a narrative.

182 Doucette, Laurel. "Family Studies as an Approach to Oral History." **Canadian Oral History Association Journal** 2 (1976/77), 24-31. The James Kealey family of Hull, Quebec recorded a collection of family folklore and oral historical memoirs which Doucette excerpted.

183 Douglass, Enid H. "Oral History." **History News** 28 (November 1973), 264. Douglass lists some hints for conducting an oral history project with the elderly.

184 _____. "Oral History and Public History." **Oral History Review** (1980), 1-5. Douglass charts the growth of the discipline of public history while noting the dearth of jobs for historians in academia. Oral history is being used as a research technique by those engaged in tracing the history of public structures.

185 Dow, Maynard Westin. "Oral History of Geography." **Professional Geographer** 26 (November 1974), 430-435. Dow's article is based on a paper delivered to the Association of American Geographers describing the Distinguished Geographer Film Interview Series. Though the enterprise was not conceived as an oral history project it has used many of the same techniques. He discusses problems which arose during and after the interviews with 57 geographers were filmed. There is a chart with the names of interviewers, interviewees, location, date and length of film.

186 Doyle, Frederick Joseph. "German Prisoners of War in the Southwestern United States During World War II: An Oral History." Doctoral dissertation, University of Denver, 1978. (Dissertation Abstracts, 39:6912-6913A). Nine German POWs who returned to America after the war and seven guards and employers were interviewed. The two groups corroborated each others' memories except in the instance of a re-education program conducted by the camp leadership.

187 "Duke University Students Learn Interviewing Techniques of 'Oral History' to Record Lives of Ordinary People." **New York Times.** May 6, 1974, p.41. A course at Duke taught by Lawrence C. Goodwin trains graduate students in oral history interviewing. Goodwin is especially interested in the lives and experiences of ordinary people in the southern U.S. He disparages some historians' reluctance to use oral history as a legitimate source of knowledge of the past.

188 Dyk, Walter. **Son of Old Man Hat: A Navaho Autobiography Recorded by Walter Dyk.** Lincoln: University of Nebraska Press, 1967. Left Handed begins his life history with his birth in 1868 and ends twenty years later. He told his story in his own language, telling a tale of tribal life in Biblical rhythms. Dyk put it into chronological order.

189 _____, and Ruth Dyk. **Left Handed: A Navajo Autobiography.** New York: Columbia University Press, 1980. This volume continues the story begun in **Son of Old Man Hat.** Left Handed begins married life and renders an almost daily account of his activities, touching on the social and cultural life of his people.

190 Ede, Lisa S. "Oral History: One Way Out of the Slough of Despond." **College Composition and Communication** 28 (December 1977), 380-382. Ede suggests a brief foray into oral history as an antidote to mid-semester slump in a college composition course.

191 Egerton, John. **Generations: An American Family.** Louisville: University of Kentucky Press, 1983. Reviewed: **Library Journal** 108 (August 1983), 1475.

192 Eiseman, Alberta. "To the Roots of Fairfield with a Recorder." **New York Times.** February 25, 1979, Section 23, p.12. The writer chronicles her part in an oral history project whose purpose was to record the history of the Westport-Norwalk area of Connecticut.

Eliades, David K., see Dial, Adolph L.

193 Eller, Ronald D. "Appalachian Oral History: New Directions for Regional Research." **Appalachian Journal** 4, #4 (1977), 2-7; Reprinted in **An Appalachian Symposium: Essays Written in Honor of Cratis D. Williams.** Jerry W. Williamson, ed. (Boone, N. Car.: Appalachian State University Press, 1977), p.2-7. Eller advocates preserving Appalachian history by collecting oral records. Some of the topics he suggests are: community and social structure; religion; race relations; and the social history of the area's major industries.

194 Ellis, Richard N. "The Duke Indian Oral History Collection at the University of New Mexico." **New Mexico History Review** 48 (July 1973), 259-263. Through the generosity of Doris Duke the University of New Mexico conducts a project aimed at recording the history of Indian life in the southwestern U.S. To the time of this writing the collection contains 338 tapes totaling 825 hours of interviews and 6400 pages of transcripts on Pueblo life and culture. Over 400 interviews are concerned with Navaho history. Material on Indian life in other parts of the country is also included in the university's archives.

195 Endersby, Elric J. "Folklore and Oral History." **New Jersey Folklore** 2, #2 (1980), 13-14.

196 Epstein, Helen. **Children of the Holocaust: Conversations with Sons and Daughters of Survivors.** New York: Putnam, 1979. Journalist Epstein was a consultant on a project which recorded the oral histories of 200 Holocaust survivors. She was the child of parents who were imprisoned in concentration camps. After

writing the final report she decided to interview the children of other survivors. She tells their stories in narrative style, interspersing the text with quotes from her subjects. While not an oral history in the accepted sense, this volume is included here because it is frequently cited in other bibliographies. Chapter 19, which is an explanation of how the book came to be written, might well be read first. There is a 16 item bibliography on the children of Holocaust survivors.

197 Eustis, Truman W., III. "Get It in Writing: Oral History and the Law." **Oral History Review** (1976), 6-18. The author, a lawyer, discusses three main areas of interest to oral historians: copyright, the right of privacy and libel. He cites several examples.

Evans, Frank B., see #3.

198 Evans, George Ewart. **The Days That We Have Seen.** London: Faber and Faber, 1975. Evans examines a village in Suffolk, discussing rural life, childhood and the work of the people. He sees a link between land use and the primary occupations of villagers, such as herring-curing. The speeches of his subjects are bridged by his narrative.

199 _____. "I Am a Tape Recorder: 'Oral History'." **Encounter** 47 (November 1976), 70, 72, 74-78. The author relates his experiences in recording interviews on tape, searching printed sources and writing up the result. In later years he turned to unedited taped interviews (see **The Edwardians**). He contrasts the techniques of American oral historians with those used in Britain for recording oral sources and utilizing oral tradition. British practitioners fortify their oral history with copious amounts of written sources. Thompson laments the destruction of the tapes and the preservation of only the typescript of the interview.

200 Evans, J.A.S. "Oral History in Herodotus." **Canadian Oral History Association Journal** 4, #2 (1980), 8-16.

201 Evanston Township High School, Senior Seminar II. **Hinky Dinks, Sundaes, and Blind Pigs: An Oral History of Evanston.** (N.p.: 1977). Reviewed: **Chicago History** 7 (Winter 1978-79), 254.

202 Fadiman, J. **An Oral History of Tribal Warfare: The Meru of Mt. Kenya.** Athens: Ohio University Press, 1982. The author conducted interviews with almost 100 warriors. He spoke with Europeans in English and with Africans in Swahili or Meru. Transcripts

are on file at the University of Nairobi. A partial
listing of participants is appended with a brief biography of each. He includes an essay on his methodology.
203 Faris, David E. "Narrative Form and Oral History: Some
Problems and Possibilities." **International Journal
of Oral History** 1 (November 1980), 159-180. Faris
examines the reasons for inaccurate oral history.
Greater care should be taken in conducting the interview and transcribing and interpreting it.
204 Farrell, Edmund. "Oral Histories as Living Literature."
English Journal 71 (April 1982), 87-92. An engaging
article by a reader hooked on fiction written in the
first person. He believes that the best published oral
histories should be considered literature of a high
order. Farrell notes that Terkel's **Working** has been
presented as drama off-Broadway. Short bibliography
of published oral histories.
205 Filippelli, Ronald L. "Oral History and the Archives."
American Archivist 39 (October 1976), 479-483. This
article is based on a paper read at the Society of
American Archivists' meeting in 1975. Filippelli believes oral historians should have interviewing skills
and subject expertise. Transcripts should be handled
like manuscripts in archival collections. Money and
proper documentation, he asserts, are the two most
important requisites for a successful, on-going project.
206 **First Person America.** Edited and with an introduction
by Ann Banks. New York: Knopf, 1980. Selected narratives collected during the 1930's as part of the WPA
Writers' Project are published here for the first time.
Persons interviewed are identified and the place
and date of the interview and the name of the tran-
scriber are noted. Several of the interviewers have
since become established American writers, e.g.
John Cheever and Ralph Ellison. Banks spoke with
some of the interviewers in preparation for this book
and quotes some of them in the introductory material.
Notes, bibliography, index.
207 Fisher, Minnie. "The Yiddishe Arbeiten Universitett:
An Oral History." **Urban Review** 9 (February 1976),
201-204. The transcript of Fisher's life history on
New York City's Lower East Side between World
Wars I and II.
208 Floyd, Candace. "Documenting History: Two Women's
Efforts to Gather the Oral History of Greenville,
Mississippi." [Reprinted from **History News.** October,

1980 issue.] **Mississippi Libraries** 45 (Spring 1981), 6-9. A popularly written article about two women who are conducting a project in Washington County, Mississippi. Photos.

209 Fonsino, Frank John. "Criteria for Evaluating Oral History Interviews." **History Teacher** 13 (February 1980), 239-243. Fonsino developed a three page form for evaluating the worth of oral history projects in the classroom. Reprinted here, the report card grades interviewing techniques, style, tape quality and typescript form and readability. He uses it as an aid in grading student projects.

210 _____. "Oral History as a Research and Teaching Tool." Doctoral dissertation, Illinois State University, 1979. (Dissertation Abstracts, 40:3939A). This study was conducted to test oral history as a research tool and a method of instruction at the college level. Fonsino concludes that oral evidence is reliable and valid, new interpretations often emerge from interviews and student attitudes were positively reinforced.

211 Fontana, Bernard L. "American Indian Oral History: An Anthropologist's Note." **History and Theory** 8, #3 (1969), 366-370. The author discusses oral history and tradition and cites ways to corroborate the testimony of the speaker. He feels that anthropologists have more in common with folklorists than with traditional historians. Oral histories of a people usually yield a more rounded picture of the culture. The definition of truth as interpreted by Indians is analyzed.

212 Foote, Edward J. "An Interview with Frederick W. Mac-Monnies, American Sculptor of the Beaux-Arts Era." **New York Historical Society Quarterly** 61 (July/October 1977), 103-123. DeWitt M. Lockman interview Mac-Monnies in 1927 as part of an ongoing series on the lives of American artists. Excerpts published here are bridged by Foote's narrative. The typescript copy was transcribed from a secretary's shorthand notes. Photos of MacMonnies' work.

213 Forman, Deborah. "Inheriting the Holocaust." **Boston** 73 (November 1981), 156-159, 213-217. Ruth Bork founded One Generation After, an organization focused on recording Holocaust history, on her return from a tour of European concentration camps. The group's main activity is an oral history project of survivors and their children. The stories of four families are summarized in the article.

214 Foronda, Marcelino A., Jr. "Oral History in the Philippines: Trends and Prospects." **International Journal of Oral History** 2 (February 1981), 13-15. Foronda has compiled a summary of work in Philippine archives and institutions. The projects focus on three main locations in the islands: the Manila area, the Visayas and Mindanao. Fox, John, see #4, 5.

215 Francis, Hywel. "The Background and Motives of Welsh Volunteers in the International Brigades, 1936-1938." **International Journal of Oral History** 2 (June 1981), 84-108. There are no written accounts by the Welsh volunteers in the Spanish Civil War but much material has been uncovered by interviewing the men, their friends and families.

216 Frank, Benis M. **Marine Corps Oral History Collection Catalog.** Rev. ed. Washington, D.C.: History Division Headquarters, U.S. Marine Corps, 1979.

217 Fraser, Linda J. "Look at Our Past: The Wellington County Oral History Project." **Canadian Oral History Association Journal** 3, #2 (1978), 25-26.

218 Fraser, Ronald. **Blood of Spain: An Oral History of the Spanish Civil War.** New York: Pantheon Books, 1979. Accounts of the Spanish Civil War by participants in five major areas of the country provide a microscopic view of the era. Daily life as endured by those not at the front is the focus here and non-Spanish citizens are excluded. The material was recorded between June, 1973, and May, 1975, in Spain and France. Fraser's prologue sets the stage for the chronological presentation of events from July, 1936 to the spring of 1939. Maps, chronology, bibliography and index. For an account of how Fraser did the research see Jim Kelly's "An Interview with Ronald Fraser." **Oral History** 8, #1 (1980), 52-57.

219 Freedman, M. Patricia, ed. "Managing Oral History Collections in the Library." **Drexel Library Quarterly** (October 1979). Freedman is editor of the issue and author of the introduction. She points out that Columbia University began preserving tapes as primary material a decade after its Oral History Office opened. She calls tapes an "audible document."

220 Freiband, Susan J., and Judy Ranney. "Some Considerations On: Oral History for Adults in the Public Library." **Catholic Library World** 51 (September 1979), 79-81. Thoughts on public libraries and oral history by two librarians. Short bibliography.

221 Friedlund, Thomas J. "Public Libraries Participating in SWLA Oral History Project." **Texas Libraries** 42 (Summer 1980), 86-89. The author names participants in the project and lists the suggestions of Oral History Association officials for successful library projects. The objectives are: better understanding of local history; training people who can subsequently aid others in conducting oral history on the local level in the Southwest; publication of a program manual for libraries.

222 Friesen, Gerhard. "Mignon in America." **Journal of German-American Studies** 14 (March 1979), 1-26.

223 Frisch, Michael. "Oral History and **Hard Times,** A Review Essay." **Oral History Review** (1979), 70-79. Frisch examines some of the book reviews garnered by Terkel's book.

224 _____, and Dorothy L. Watts. "Oral History and the Presentation of Class Consciousness: **The New York Times** Versus the Buffalo Unemployed." **International Journal of Oral History** 1, #2 (1980), 88-110. Buffalo's unemployed were examined in 1974-75 by students in the American Studies Program at the city's SUNY campus. A controversy over the editing of the material collected developed. The article discusses the conflicts.

225 Fry, Amelia R. "Nine Commandments of Oral History." **Journal of Library History** 3 (January 1968), 63-73. This amusing article is written as a neophyte's interview of an experienced oral historian. The sage tours some of the pits into which his colleagues have tumbled.

226 _____. "Reflections on Ethics." **Oral History Review** (1975), 16-28. Fry discusses the Oral History Association's Goals and Guidelines which mandate the responsibilities of the researcher, the interviewee and the sponsoring institution.

227 _____. "Suffragist Alice Paul's Memoirs: Pros and Cons of Oral History." **Frontiers** 2, #2 (1977) 82-86. The author conducted two marathon sessions with Alice Paul and uses them as a springboard in considering issues in oral history. She examines the uniqueness of the movement and its similarities with other historical methods; its validity and some of the major problems confronting it.

228 _____, and Willa Baum. "A Janus Look at Oral History." **American Archivist** 32 (October 1969), 319-326. Written on the eve of the Fourth Colloquium on Oral History, the article lists some ongoing projects.

Goals and Guidelines promulgated by the Oral History Association in 1969 are reproduced verbatim and commented upon. Recurring questions concern the establishment of a workable relationship between interlocutor and subject; editing of transcripts; tape erasure after transcription; and the constant problem of funding.

_____, see also Baum, Willa.

229 Gallagher, Dorothy. **Hannah's Daughters: Six Generations of an American Family, 1876-1976.** New York: Crowell, 1976. This is the oral history of a white, working class family in Michigan and Washington state. It is the result of six weeks of conversations with women of the pseudonymous Lambersons in 1974. Gallagher welds their speeches together with background information, family photos and genealogical charts. Afterword by Robert Coles.

230 Gamio, Manuel. **The Life Story of the Mexican Immigrant: Autobiographic Documents.** (Reprint of the University of Chicago Press edition of 1931 entitled **The Mexican Immigrant: His Life Story.**) New introduction by Paul S. Taylor. New York: Dover, 1971. Seventy-six Mexican immigrants interviewed by anthropologist Gamio are identified. Interviews are arranged by topic: leaving Mexico; the experiences of Indians, mestizos, the middle class, women; assimilation; religion.

231 Garcia, Mario T. "Chicano History: An Oral History Approach." **Journal of San Diego History** 23 (Winter 1977), 46-53. Garcia recaps the reasons for Mexican immigration to U.S. labor markets. Excerpts from four interviews are reprinted. An afterword points up discrepancies between what the subjects said and incidents which are documented.

Gardner, A. Dudley, see **An Oral History of Northwestern Colorado**

Gaskin, J.M., see Charlton, Thomas L.

232 Gebhard, Krysztof M., ed. **The Saskatchewan Oral History Conference 1981 Proceedings.** Regina: Saskatchewan Archives Board, 1981. Some of the topics of the papers presented are: oral history and folklore; oral history in museums and archives; its use in the classroom; interviewing; and local history.

233 Gentile, Karlene. "Nine Plain-spoken Lives: An Oral History Project with Older Adults." **Show-Me Libraries** 33 (May 1982), 22-26. Excerpts from Jerred Metz's **Drinking the Dipper Dry**, a collection of oral testimony by adults in the St. Louis, Missouri area.

234 Gerard, Helene. "Remembrance of Things Past—Orally." **New York Library Association Bulletin** 26 (March 1978), 1, 8-9. Gerard briefly covers the main points of doing oral history for the beginner. She illustrates with examples from her experience with her Orthodox Jewish family.

Gerritsen, Rolf, see Docker, Ted.

235 Gibson, Douglas M. "Oral History: A Publisher's Perspective." **Canadian Oral History Association Journal** 4, #2 (1980), 1-8. Gibson discusses publishers' criteria for selecting and editing oral histories and how questions of procedure and ethics are handled. He illustrates his points with examples from publications by Macmillan of Canada.

236 Gibson, Michael D. "A Methodological Overview of Oral History." **Annals of Iowa** 44 (Spring 1979), 639-653. Gibson writes a brief history of the movement, mentioning several projects. Release forms and sample data sheets are reprinted. He covers techniques and conduct of the interview. Because the atmosphere of the interview and its nuances cannot be captured on paper, he urges retention of the tape.
_____, see also #6.

237 Gilinsky, Rhoda M. "A Program to Honor State's Suffragist Pioneers." **New York Times.** April 25, 1982, Section 23, p.2. Gilinsky reports on the University of Connecticut's project entitled "The Political Activities of the First Generation of Fully Enfranchised Connecticut Women, 1920-1945." A series of five programs for Public Radio was based on the tapes. Interviewees were 21 women, aged 64 to 100, active in the state's political arena, social welfare and reform.

238 Gilmour, Andrew. **My Role in the Rehabilitation of Singapore: 1946-1953.** Singapore: Institute of Southeast Asian Studies, 1973. (Oral History Pilot Study, No. 2). The transcript of an interview with a British Colonial Secretary charged with reconstructing Singapore's economy after World War II.

239 Glass, Mary E. **The Oral History Project of the Center for Western North American Studies: A Bibliography.** Reno: Desert Research Institute, University of Nevada, 1968.

240 Gluck, Sherna. "Interlude or Change: Women and the World War II Work Experience." **International Journal of Oral History** 3 (June 1982), 92-113. Gluck examined the histories of 43 women who worked during the

second war and were affected by the experience in later years.

241 _____. "What's So Special About Women? Women's Oral History." **Frontiers** 2, #2 (1977), 3-17. Gluck introduces an issue of **Frontiers** devoted to women's oral history. She discusses the special problems of achieving rapport between interviewer and speaker and cautions against some common errors.

242 Goffee, Robert E. "The Butty System and the Kent Coalfield." **Society for the Study of Labour History** [Great Britain] #34 (1977), 41-55. Goffee reviews and prints extracts from interviews with sons, fathers and grandfathers in the mining community of Aylesham. Union activity, the Depression and a system of subcontracting are some of the topics.

243 Gold, Don. **Until the Singing Stops: A Celebration of Life and Old Age in America.** New York: Holt, Rinehart and Winston, 1979. Gold's book is made up of the edited transcripts of interviews with twenty Americans aged 65 and older. A photograph and short biography introduces each speaker, some of whom are well-known, i.e., Dr. Mary Calderone of SIECUS.

244 Goldman, Harry Merton. "Pins and Needles: An Oral History." Doctoral dissertation, New York University, 1977. (Dissertation Abstracts, 38:7028A). **Pins and Needles** was a left wing, satirical revue staged by the International Ladies Garment Workers' Union in 1937. The original cast and audience were union members but its success led to an Actors Equity production which ran for 1108 performances. Fifty former cast members were interviewed by Goldman. He presents the material in chronological order and includes brief biographies of cast and crew.

245 _____. "Workers Theatre to Broadway Hit: The Evolution of an American Radical Revue." **Oral History** 10 (Spring 1982), 56-66. This article is based on material gathered by the author for his dissertation. (See previous entry.)

Goldman, Richard, see Lehane, Stephen.

246 Goulbourne, Harry. "Oral History and Black Labour in Britain: An Overview." **Oral History** 8 (Spring 1980), 24-34. Goulbourne opposes the common view that blacks began coming to Britain in 1948. He dates their arrival to the 1880's and shows how oral history can be used to verify his contention and supplement written sources.

247 Goulding, Stuart D. "The McDonald Interviews." **History Today** 29 (July 1979), 429-440. Judge James McLean McDonald conducted 407 interviews of Revolutionary War participants from 1844 to 1851 in Westchester and Fairfield counties, New York. He questioned 241 men and women aged 70 to 108 years. Goulding presents excerpts and makes explanatory comments.

248 Graham, Stanley. "The Lancashire Textile Project: A Description of the Work and Some of the Techniques Involved." **Oral History** 8 (Autumn 1980), 48-52. The project was devoted to gathering a social history of textile workers and members of the surrounding community. The technology of the industry was also investigated. Graham discusses some of the problems which arose in the course of the project and methods of funding.

Grainger, Bruce, see #7.

Greenebaum, Frances, see Kachaturoff, Grace.

249 Grele, Ronald J. "Can Anyone Over Thirty Be Trusted: A Friendly Critique of Oral History." **Oral History Review** (1978), 36-44. Grele sees two major problems with the field: bibliographic control of tapes and transcripts; and evaluation of the worth of what is produced.

250 _____, ed. **Envelopes of Sound: Six Practitioners Discuss the Method, Theory and Practice of Oral History and Oral Testimony.** Chicago: Precedent Publishers, 1975. The outgrowth of a 1973 meeting of the Organization of American Historians, this collection is aimed at the layperson. Studs Terkel, Jan Vansina, Saul Benison, Dennis Tedlock, Alice Kessler Harris and the editor discuss the problems of doing oral history.

251 _____. "Listen to Their Voices: Two Case Studies in the Interpretation of Oral History Interviews." **Oral History** 7 (1979), 33-42. Grele examines "the particular vision of history articulated in an interview." He believes interviewing "is actually a process in the construction of a usable past."

252 _____. "A Personal Sampler from The Seventh National Coloquium on Oral History." **Journal of Library History** 8 (January 1973), 40-41. The author's opinions of some of the speakers and panels at the 7th colloquium.

253 _____. "Surmisable Variety: Interdisciplinarity and Oral Testimony." **American Quarterly** 27 (August 1975), 275-295. Grele discusses the interplay of oral

history with other disciplines such as linguistics and anthropology, focusing on the interview itself. He urges linguistic and literary analyses of the interview. Problems of interview theory and methodology are covered in depth. The 59 extensive notes include many bibliographical references.
_____, see also #8.

254 Griffiths, Tom. "The Debate About Oral History." **Melbourne History Journal** [Australia] 13 (1981), 16-21. Griffiths discusses disagreements between traditional historians and oral historians.

255 Gross, Franklin S. "Enfield's Excited About Living History." **Senior Scholastic: Scholastic Teacher** 94 (May 9, 1969), 13-14. The author helped develop a Living History Center in his high school using oral history techniques. Current events rather than the past is stressed. Color slides record projects, such as the building of a new school in the community.

256 Hackman, Larry J. "Oral History and the Consumer Interest." **Oral History Review** (1978), 55-58. Hackman sees "consumers" as those who use the tapes and transcripts of a particular project. He has some suggestions for evaluating the material in order to upgrade the product.

257 Hackney Workers' Education Association. **Working Lives.** London: Centerprise, 1976-77.

258 Haines, David. **Tape Recording Local History.** London: Print and Press Services, 1977.

259 Halas, George. **Halas By Halas: The Autobiography of George Halas With Gwen Morgan and Arthur Veysey.** New York: McGraw-Hill, 1979. Two **Chicago Tribune** correspondents transcribed this life history of Halas, owner of the Bears football team. "Papa Bear" talks about his early years and his lifelong involvement with football. The text appears to be a straight transcription. There is no explanation of taping or editing procedures. Roster of Chicago Bears players, coaches. Photos, index.

260 Haley, Alex. **Autobiography of Malcolm X.** New York: Grove Press, 1964. **Roots** author Haley worked with Malcolm X on this autobiography. The Black Muslim leader submitted to a series of interviews with Haley. This transcription is edited from notes and tapes. The epilogue is an integral part of the story, containing an account of Malcolm X's assassination. Rosengarten's **All God's Chilren** (q.v.) is in some ways a parallel to this book.

261 _____. "Black History, Oral History, and Genea-
    logy." **Oral History Review** (1973), 1-25. This article
    is extracted from the Seventh Annual Colloquium
    held in 1972. Haley chronicles his search for his African
    slave ancestor which led to the publication of **Roots.**
262 Hall, Jacquelyn Dowd. "Documenting Diversity: The
    Southern Experience." **Oral History Review** (1976),
    19-28. The author sees oral history as a way to replace
    the diaries which most people no longer keep. She
    describes the Southern Oral History Program in Chapel
    Hill, North Carolina. Gathering material for future
    scholars is one of the program's main purposes.
263 _____. "Oral History Movement: Seeking Out the
    Voices of Women, Blacks, Radicals, and Workers
    for a Better-balanced Story." **South Today** 4 (April
    1973), 2-3. Hall describes several current projects
    in the southern U.S.: Fisk University's Black Oral
    History Program; The Civil Rights Documentation
    Project; the Institute for Southern Studies. All are
    designed to combat the "Great White Man" theory
    of history.
264 Hamburger, Robert. **Our Portion of Hell, Fayette County,
    Tennessee: An Oral History of the Struggle for Civil
    Rights.** New York: Links, 1973. Fayette County, with
    a population that is 60% black, is the third poorest
    county in the U.S. Hamburger worked there in the
    Civil Rights Movement since 1965. He recorded the
    interviews presented here in 1971 and 1972. Speakers
    are identified and most include some biographical
    information in their tapes.
265 Hammer, Kenneth, ed. "Notes From the Custer Battle-
    field. Walter Mason Camp's Interviews with Survivors
    of the Little Bighorn." **American West** 13 (March-April
    1976), 36-45. Hammer excerpts material from Camp's
    interviews with 60 Seventh Cavalry survivors and
    150 Indians. A complete transcription was published
    by BYU Press (1976) and is titled **Custer in '76, Walter
    Camp's Notes on the Custer Fight.**
266 Hand, Samuel B., ed. "William E. Brown, Dean of UVM's
    Medical College, 1945-52: An Oral History Interview."
    Vermont History 41 (Summer 1973), 158-172. Hand
    uses excerpts from material recorded by Paul Kendall
    French detailing Brown's service in Greece as a public
    health administrator during World War II and in the
    period of the Greek Civil War.
    _____, see also #9.

267 Handfield, F. Gerald, Jr. "The Importance of Video History in Libraries." **Drexel Library Quarterly** 15 (October 1979), 29-34. The author defines video history as an interview "preserved by an audio and a video signal." He believes it offers a way of keeping a record of body language and tone of voice. He discusses library policies of acquisition and preservation of video interviews. Short bibliography.

268 Hareven, Tamara K. "Search for Generational Memory: Tribal Rites in Industrial Society." **Daedalus** 107 (Fall 1978), 137-149. Hareven defines "generational memory" as individuals' remembrances of their own family history. She discusses Haley's **Roots** and links it to the oral tradition of the African griot. The role of the interview itself and its influence on what is recalled is contrasted with oral traditions in nonliterate societies. 26 notes with bibliographical references.

269 _____, and Randolph Langenbach. **Amoskeag: Life and Work in an American Factory-city.** New York: Pantheon Books, 1978. The Amoskeag Company in Manchester, New Hampshire, was, in the early part of this century, the largest textile mill in the world. In operation from 1838 to 1936, it was always head-quartered in Boston. Initially, the largest part of its labor force was made up of unmarried females from rural New England. These interviews evolved from two separate studies conducted by the authors. Introductory chapters on the history of Amoskeag and textile making are lucidly presented. Speakers are introduced and identified. Photos of the mill, its workers and the interviewees make this volume a stand-out among oral histories.

270 Harkell, Gina. "The Migration of Mining Families to the Kent Coalfield Between the Wars." **Oral History** 6 (Spring 1978), 98-113. Harkell quotes miners on the conditions in Kentish mines but turns to women for the majority of her material. Speakers are identified in the notes.

271 Harlan, Robert D. "Review Article: Oral Histories of San Francisco Printing." **Library Quarterly** 45 (April 1975), 202-205. **Books and Printing in the San Francisco Bay Area** is the work of Ruth Teiser, an associate of Berkeley's Regional Oral History Office. Twenty-five interviews comprise the series. Abridged versions of eight interviews are available in **Printing as a Performing Art,** edited by Teiser and Catherine Harroun

(Book Club of California, 1970). Complete bibliographical information on the transcripts is listed.
Harlow, Richard R., see Beasley, Maurine.
272 Harris, Iverson L. "Reminiscences of Lomaland: Madame
Tingley and the Theosophical Institute of San Diego."
San Diego History 20 (Summer 1974), 1-32.
273 Harris, James A. "Speaking of History: Oral History
in the Classroom." **Learning** 7 (October 1978), 72-74.
The author believes the teaching of facts doesn't
prepare children adequately to deal with life but
that they should be taught to work independently.
He lists guidelines for a successful project and some
methods for keeping the interest of younger pupils
alive.
274 Harris, Raymond, M.D., and Sara Harris. "Therapeutic
Uses of Oral History Techniques in Medicine." **International Journal of Aging and Human Development**
12, #1 (1980/1981), 27-34. Oral history techniques
are used by Harris in the practice of clinical medicine
to supplement routine medical history.
275 Harrison, Alexander. "An Oral History Approach to
the Study of the Counter-revolution in Algeria, 1954-
1962." Doctoral dissertation, New York University,
1980. (Dissertation Abstracts, 41:2722A). Harrison
interviewed lower echelon members of the Organisation
Armee Secrete for their version of the French defeat
in Algeria.
276 Harrison, Alferdteen. **Piney Woods School: An Oral
History.** Jackson, University Press of Mississippi,
1982. The Mississippi school was founded to give
rural blacks a practical, vocational education. This
is a biography of the institution from its beginnings
in 1909. Though billed as an oral history, the book
contains more straight narrative than transcribed
oral history.
277 Harrison, Lowell H. "Recollections of Some Tennessee
Slaves." **Tennessee Historical Quarterly** 33 (Summer
1974), 175-190. An overview of the WPA slave interviews conducted with blacks living in the state. Topics
commented on include food, clothing, housing, punish-
ment and religion.
278 Hart, Carroll. "The New Documentation: Oral History
and Photography." **Drexel Library Quarterly** 15 (October
1979), 5-11. Hart urges the preservation of photos
to supplement oral history. He cites some instances
in which their discovery led to significant finds.

279 Hasdorff, James C. "Sources in Aerospace History: The USAF Oral History Collection." **Aerospace Historian** 23 (June 1976), 103-104. Hasdorff discusses the ongoing Air Force program which began as an investigation into air power in Southeast Asia. The high value of the resulting interviews led to its becoming a permanent project. Biographical interviews with military personnel and civilians are the chief component. Names of some prominent individuals are listed.

280 Hastings, Robert J. "Oral History: Baptists in Their Everyday Clothes." **Baptist History and Heritage** 11 (April 1976), 80-83. Hastings relates how the workshop of the Southern Baptist Historical Commission on Oral History led to the writing of his book **We Were There: An Oral History of the Illinois Baptist State Association.** He covers the interviewing, what he would do differently were he repeating the project, and the marketing of the finished product.

281 Hatch, James V. "Retrieving Black Theatre History or Mouth to Mouth Resuscitation." **Black Scholar** 10 (July 1979), 58-61. Hatch is associated with the Hatch-Billops Collection which contains over six hundred tapes. He makes a plea for the interviewing of black performers in all phases of entertainment.

Hatcher, Barbara A., see Olson, Mary.

282 Hay, Cynthia. "The Pangs of the Past." **Oral History** 9 (Spring 1981), 41-46. Hay challenges the presumption that only "comfortable topics" are recalled accurately. She examines current work by psychologists on memory.

Healy, Dermot, see Bundy, Colin.

283 Heiges, Mary J. "To Tape or Not to Tape: That Is the Question on Tape." **Minnesota Libraries** 24 (Winter 1974-1975), 199-204. In this article Heiges makes some general recommendations for carrying out an oral history project, interpolating notes on the particular practices of the Hopkins (Minnesota) Public Library. Supplies, funding, who and how to interview are covered.

Heizer, Robert F., see Blinman, Eric.

Helm, Mike, see Lockley, Fred.

284 Henige, David. "Day Was of Sudden Turned into Night: On the Use of Eclipses for Dating Oral History." **Comparative Studies in Society and History** 18 (October 1976), 476-501. A summary of various attempts to date events whose reference point is eclipses. Instances

in China, medieval Europe and Africa in written and
oral history contexts are examined. Henige points
out the pitfalls by citing difficulties with the word
"eclipse" which doesn't always denote what a twentieth
century speaker of English perceives as its meaning.
285 _____. **Oral Historiography.** New York: Longman,
1982. The author narrowly defines oral history and
oral tradition showing how medieval English chroniclers
used oral sources in their writings. The major portion
of the book is concerned with collecting oral tradition
in Third World countries, covering topics such as
the language barrier and getting along with local
officials. Henige critiques (pp. 116-118) the WPA
Writers' Project interviews with ex-slaves. This is
a well-done, unpedantic discussion.
286 Henderson, Joyce. "Oral History Goes to School." **Social
Studies Review** 15 (February 1975), 10-12, 41. Henderson gives examples of the use of oral history in high
school curriculums.
287 Henry, R. "Oral History: A Strategy." **Senior Scholastic**
113 Teachers Edition (January 9, 1981), 1.
288 Herrera-Sobek, Maria. **The Bracero Experience: Elitelore
Versus Folklore.** Los Angeles, UCLA Latin American
Center, 1979. The author examines the lives of Bra-
ceros, Mexicans who came to work in the U.S. under
PL 78 between 1951 and 1964. Chapter Two "An Oral
History Interview with a Composite Bracero" is the
product of her several hundred hours of talking with
laborers in Huecorio, Mexico, about their experiences.
289 Hill, Charles C. "Oral History and the History of Canadian
Art." **Canadian Oral History Association Journal**
2 (1976-77), 31-35. Hill used tapes in preparing for
an exhibit at the National Gallery of Canada. He
discusses how oral history and art history can benefit
from each other.
Hirsch, Jerrold, see Terrill, Tom E.
290 "Historian Helps Corporations Recall the Story of Their
Past." **New York Times** May 26, 1980, Section 4,
p. 2. Mimi Stein, formerly with the Bancroft Library's
Regional Oral History Office, founded Oral History
Associates to record corporate histories. She is paid
a consultant's fee by the company to interview former
employees on corporate history.
291 Hoffman, Abraham. "A Note on the Field Research
Interviews of Paul S. Taylor for Mexican Labor in
the United States Monographs." **Pacific Historian**

20 (Summer 1976), 123-131. Eighty per cent of the interviews conducted by Dr. Taylor from 1927 to 1930 were never published. They are edited and on deposit in the University of California's Bancroft Library. The location of the interviews, their number and notes on the interviewees are listed in this article.

292 Hoffman, Alice M. "Oral History in the United States." **Journal of Library History** 7 (July 1972), 277-284. An overview of oral history in this country with particular attention to the author's involvement in the United Steelworkers of America project at Pennsylvania State University.

293 _____. "Reliability and Validity in Oral History." **Today's Speech** 22 (Winter 1974), 23-27. Hoffman provides an overview of some current projects and lists guidelines for oral history interviews set forth by the Oral History Association. She deals with the problem of ascertaining the truth of what the interviewee says pointing out that he can be asked direct questions to resolve discrepancies with the written record. Because underlings write many of the documents which government officials sign, Hoffman believes that the true author is not always known.

294 Holden, Len. "'Think of Me Simply as the Skipper': Industrial Relations at Vauxhalls 1920-1950." **Oral History** 9 (Autumn 1981), 19-32. Holden investigated labor relations at Vauxhalls, a British auto manufacturer, through interviews with workers after being stonewalled by management. The result was a picture which was not as tranquil as he had been led to believe initially.

295 Holles, Everett R. "Nixon Foundation Speeds Start on Coast Library and Museum." **New York Times** August 11, 1974, p. 43. Holles mentions in passing that the oral history tapes made by Whittier College, the former president's alma mater, will be housed in the library.

296 Holman, Barbara D. **Oral History Collection of the Forest History Society: An Annotated Guide.** Santa Cruz, Calif.: Forest History Society, 1976. This is a guide to the interviews collected since 1952 by the society. The main body is arranged by interviewee listing: subjects discussed, interviewer's name, date of interview, restrictions on the material. Subject index.

297 Holmes, H.T. "Oral History in the Mississippi Department of Archives and History." **Journal of Mississippi History**

38 (February 1976), 111-117. The interviews in the
department's collection are listed alphabetically
with a brief description of their contents and availa-
bility.
298 _____. "Oral History in the Mississippi Department
of Archives and History." **Journal of Mississippi History**
39 (February 1977), 83-88. Continues the listing begun
in the February 1976 issue.
299 Holway, John. **Voices from the Great Black Baseball
Leagues.** New York: Dodd, Mead, 1975. Holway deplores
in his introduction the absence of information on
the Black Leagues in the Baseball Hall of Fame exhibits
at Cooperstown, New York. His opening chapter is
a sketch of the history of these leagues. Taped interviews with the stars of black baseball make up the
rest of the book. Cool Papa Bell, Pee Wee Butts,
Willie Wells and Crush Holloway are some of the
subjects. Photos and statistics of the leagues are
appended.
300 Hoopes, James. **Oral History: An Introduction for Students.** Chapel Hill, University of North Carolina Press,
1979. Hoopes' volume is an excellent handbook for
all practitioners of oral history from high school
students to the professional historian. The opening
chapter places the movement in historical context.
Succeeding chapters, titled "Personality," "Culture,"
and "Society" treat their relation to oral history.
The interview is dealt with from initial contact with
the subject to the handling of the transcript. The
bibliography is limited to titles mentioned in the
text and footnotes.
301 Hoopes, Roy. **Americans Remember the Homefront:
An Oral Narrative.** New York: Hawthorn, 1977. Hoopes
conducted conversations with Americans who lived
the years 1941 to 1945 as civilians in the U.S. The
result was 700,000 words which he excerpts here.
He uses the subtitle "oral narrative" to distinguish
the work from oral history in an academic sense.
The extracts are arranged into a narrative covering
life in Washington, D.C., industry, the experiences
of wives and children and several other topics. A
concluding portion describes people's feelings about
Truman's assumption of the presidency.
302 _____. "Taped Talk: Storing Tomorrow's Source Materials." **High Fidelity** 27 (August 1977), 61-65. The
author confuses oral history with taped interviews,
mentioning several published works of each type.

303 Hoover, Herbert T. "Oral History in the United States."
In **The Past Before Us: Contemporary Historical Writing
in the United States**, Michael Kammen, ed. (Ithaca:
Cornell University Press, 1980), p.391-407. Hoover
cites the work of Herodotus and de las Casas as fore-
runners of the movement. The work of the Forest
History Society and Nevins' initial forays into interviewing are chronicled. By 1966 about ninety groups
existed for the purpose of compiling oral history
material. A redirection of the movement in the late
1960's led to interviews with non-elites and expansion
to include members of minorities in American life.
Criteria for evaluating projects and publications
are: specific goals; funding; adequately trained interviewers; proper preparation for the interview; processing of the tapes; and the legal rights of the participants.
Several published oral histories are briefly noted
and commented upon.
_____, see also Cash, Joseph H.

304 Horn, Stanley F., and Charles W. Crawford. "Perspectives
on Southern Forestry: The **Southern Lumberman**,
Industrial Forestry, and Trade Associations." **Journal
of Forest History** 21 (January 1977), 18-30. Interview
transcript.

305 Hotchkiss, Ron. "Oral History in the Classroom." **History
and Social Science Teacher** 14 (Spring 1979), 205-213.
The author outlines a unit on oral history dealing
with the 1930's Depression in Canada. He believes
the interviews created empathy between the elderly
subjects and his students. Bibliography.

306 Hoyle, Norman. "Oral History." **Library Trends** 21 (July
1972), 60-82. Hoyle believes the purpose of the interview "is to create new archival material for other
writers to use." He distinguishes three types of programs: autobiographical memoirs; biographical material; and those centering around an event or topic.
The controversy over the choice of the interviewer,
whether a professional historian or trained layperson,
is discussed. This is an excellent overview of the
whole movement. 45 references.

307 Hubner, Mary. "Drama Based on Oral Tradition." **History
News** 36 (June 1981), 12-16. Hubner reports on three
dramatic productions in Baltimore; Whitesburg, Kentucky; and St. Paul, Minnesota. "Baltimore Voices"
is the edited transcript of 7000 pages of material
in which people talk about their neighborhoods,

families, work and the Depression. The Kentucky presentation is organized around "yarns." In St. Paul, Lance Belville used oral history techniques in gathering material for his scripts dealing with aspects of the history of the Twin Cities.

308 Hughes, Gary K. "Fifth Annual Canadian Oral History Association Conference." **Canadian Oral History Association Journal** 4, #1 (1979), 31-36. The theme of the 1978 Toronto conference was oral history and education.

309 _____. "Report of the Canadian Oral History Conference in Montreal, June 2-4, 1980." **Canadian Oral History Association Journal** 4, #2 (1980), 35-45. Speakers at the conference covered a wide range of topics, among them: general thoughts on the whole movement; immigration; interviewing; current work in the U.S. and Africa; social and labor history.

310 Humez, Jean M., and Laurie Crumpacker. "Oral History in Teaching Women's Studies." **Oral History Review** (1979), 53-69. The authors, instructors at Boston area colleges, outline different life history projects their students carried out with women in the community and their own female relatives. They see the movement as an excellent method for filling the gaps in the written record of women's history.

311 Humphreys, Hubert. **Louisiana Oral History Collections: A Directory.** Shreveport, La.: LSU-Shreveport Book Store, 1980. The directory is arranged alphabetically by person, collection name and subject heading with many cross references. The interviewer's name and the date and length of each item are listed. Main entries include a description of the topics covered.

312 _____. "Oral History Research in Louisiana: An Overview." **Louisiana History** 20 (Fall 1979), 353-371. Humphreys cites three types of programs: 1) research projects by professional historians; 2) on-going archival research projects; 3) folk history or cultural heritage projects. Louisiana has several archives of verbatim typescripts of interviews conducted in the 1930's. The greater part of the article is on past and current use of oral history by the state's historians.

313 Humphries, Stephen. **Hooligans or Rebels: An Oral History of Working Class Childhood and Youth 1889-1939.** Oxford: Blackwell, 1981. Oral history archives at the University of Essex, Manchester Polytechnic and the Avon County Reference Library provided

Humphries with material for this study. He prints selections from material in the three collections to underpin his thesis. Pranks, family life, street gangs and reformatories are some of the topics.

314 _____. "Steal to Survive: The Social Crime of Working Class Children 1890-1940." **Oral History** 9 (Spring 1981), 24-33. Humphries discusses petty crimes perpetrated by children and buttresses his thoughts with excerpts from interviews.

315 Husband, Michael B. "Reflections on Teaching American Indian History." **Journal of American Indian Education** 16 (January 1977), 7-14. Husband gives an overview of Indian history as written by whites. He lists several oral history programs in progress at the time of this writing.

316 Hutchins, Frances. "Why Oral History? (A Rationale)." **Bay State Librarian** 71 (Spring 1982), 16-20. Hutchins, writes a standard introduction to the movement and describes the Simmons Library School course on oral history. The interview transcripts were indexed and classified in such a way as to make them easily available to future users.

317 Huwiler, Paul. "Keeping Yesterday the Way It Is." **Connecticut Libraries** 23 (Fall 1981), 30-31. An introductory article with a checklist for organizing a project.

Hyde, Michael J., see Clark, E. Culpepper.

318 Ilisevich, Robert D. "Oral History in Undergraduate Research." **History Teacher** 6 (November 1972), 47-50. The author suggests oral history projects as an alternative to the research paper for undergraduates. He briefly outlines a program his students at Alliance College undertook to interview members of the local Polish American community.

319 Indiana University. Libraries. **Guide to Indiana University Oral History Research Projects and Related Studies.** Bloomington: Indiana University, 1977.

320 Ingram, Anne G. "An Oral History Study of the Women's Equity Movement, University of Maryland, College Park (1968-1978)." **Maryland Historian** 9 (Fall 1978), 1-25. A prologue to the article provides background information on the status of women in the U.S. and on the Maryland campus in particular. Pseudonyms are used though biographical information is sketched. Discrimination against women in tenure, pay and advancement are the focus of the excerpts quoted here.

321 "Interview with John T. Mason, Jr., Director of Oral History at the U.S. Naval Institute." **U.S. Naval Institute Proceedings** 99 (July 1973), 42-47. The transcript of this interview includes a lengthy digression of the Vice Admiral Herbert D. Riley interview transcript. A bibliography of oral history material available c.1973 or to be released shortly by the Institute is appended.

322 Ireland, Florence. "The Northeast Archives of Folklore and Oral History: A Brief Description and Catalog of Its Holdings, 1958-1972." **Northeast Folklore** 13 (1971), 3-86. This is an annotated catalog of the archive at the University of Maine. When the collection began in 1958 the emphasis was on folklore of Maine and the eastern provinces of Canada. In later years material on the work and recreation of the area's inhabitants gathered through oral history interviews was emphasized.

323 Irving, Baiba. "Oral History 75." **Politics** [Australia] 10 (November 1975), 155-157. Summarizes the proceedings of a conference held at LaTrobe University in 1975 and reports on current work in Australia.

324 Isichei, Elizabeth. **Igbo Worlds: An Anthology of Oral Histories and Historical Descriptions.** London: Macmillan, 1977. The histories presented here were chosen for their typicality. The author's students collected them in their home areas. Some life histories are included. A final chapter covers African oral history listing techniques for obtaining, recording and transmitting the material.

325 Ives, Edward D. "Pitfalls in Oral History Programs." **Maine Historical Society Quarterly** 13, #4 (1974), 204-215. Ives lists as pitfalls: inadequate interview preparation; being unfamiliar with the equipment; too much informality; limiting interviews to the elite; and not transcribing tapes.

326 _____. **The Tape-recorded Interview: A Manual for Field Workers in Folklore and Oral History.** Rev. and enl. ed. Knoxville: University of Tennessee Press, 1980. 1974 ed. titled **A Manual for Field Workers.** This publication grew from the author's classroom outline for teaching novice "foxfirers" how to collect and preserve interview material. He emphasizes that the interview itself is worthless if proper preparation is not made. The functioning of tape recorders and the processing of transcripts is covered in detail.

Annotated bibliography, index, samples of release
forms and interview transcripts.
327 "JFK at the Summit: Kremlinologist View on First Ken-
nedy-Khrushchev Encounter." **Newsweek** 76 (September
7, 1970), 32-33. A brief account of tapes by George
F. Kennan, Charles E. Bohlen and Llewellyn Thompson
concerning the summit conference between Kennedy
and Khrushchev in Vienna in 1961.
328 "JFK Tapes: How It Was." **Newsweek** 76 (August 31,
1970), 23-24, 29. This article touches briefly on the
more controversial of the 300 tapes made by Kennedy's
friends and enemies.
329 Jacques, Joseph W. "Recollections and Reflections
of Professors of Adult Education: Early 20th Century
Leaders and Pioneers in the Field." Doctoral dissertation, Florida State University, 1973. (Dissertation
Abstracts: 34:3812-13A). Jacques taped interviews
with several adult educators concerning their philosophies of education. A number of different themes
emerged from the talks. All the subjects believed
that education is an on-going process and urged the
public be made aware that learning continues throughout one's life.
330 Janiewski, Dolores. "'Sisters under Their Skins?': The
Effects of Race Upon the Efforts of Women Tobacco
Workers to Organize in Durham, North Carolina."
Oral History 7, #2 (1979), 31-41. The author interviewed
black and white women for information on union
activities. She found segregation the rule even after
retirement. People who left the company were reluc-
tant to speak for fear of repercussions on relatives
still employed.
331 Jehs, Randall W. "A Survey of Oral History Collections
in Indiana." **Indiana Magazine of History** 68 (December
1972), 315-337. The body of the article is a list of
the holdings of various Indiana libraries and organizations which collect and maintain oral history material.
Individuals who were interviewed are named and
identified by occupation or time period.
Jenkins, Sara, see **Past, Present.**
332 Jensen, Joan, Beverly Baca, and Barbara Bolin. "Family
History and Oral History." **Frontiers** 2, #2 (1977),
93-97. Jensen teaches women's history at New Mexico
State University. Her students used oral history techniques to record the history of their mothers and
grandmothers. Baca's and Bolin's interviews are excerpted.

333 Jensen, Richard. "Oral History, Quantification and the New Social History." **Oral History Review** 9 (1981), 13-25. Jensen recaps how social scientists and pollsters employ sampling and enjoins oral historians to go and do likewise.
_____, see also Campbell, D'Ann.

334 Johns, Brenda B. **Black Oral History In Nebraska: A Handbook for Researchers and Students of Oral Traditions in Black Communities.** Omaha: University of Nebraska Press, 1980. Reviewed **North Dakota History** 48 (Spring 1981), 38-39.

335 Johnson, Cynthia Jean. "A New Life: The Iowa Coal Mines." **Palimpsest** 56 (March-April 1975), 56-64. A transcript of the author's interview with John Corso, aged 76, who immigrated to Iowa from Italy in 1914. Photos.

336 Jones, Alden H. **From Jamestown to Coffin Rock: A History of Weyerhaueser Operations in Southwest Washington.** Tacoma: Weyerhaueser Co., 1974. Reviewed: **Journal of Forest History** 19 (July 1975), 145-146.

337 Jones, Merfyn. "Welsh Immigrants in the Cities of North West England 1890-1930: Some Oral Testimony." **Oral History** 9, #2 (Autumn 1981), 33-41. Jones used oral evidence to document Welsh culture and beliefs. Ignored by both English and Welsh historians, there tends to be little documentation of their enclaves in Liverpool and Manchester.

338 Jordan, Julia A. "Oklahoma's Oral History Collection: New Source for Indian History." **Chronicles of Oklahoma** 49 (Summer 1971), 150-172. This University of Oklahoma project is part of the larger effort sponsored by Miss Doris Duke. She donated money to several western schools to foster programs for gathering primary documents of Indian history. Interviewers with a background of working with Indians tape the material. Excerpts from various interviews are reprinted. Photos.
Joseph, Herman, see Courtwright, David T.

339 Joseph, Peter. **Good Times: An Oral History of America in the Nineteen-sixties.** New York: Charterhouse, 1973. An outgrowth of the author's senior thesis at Princeton, these interview excerpts are presented in a rough chronological order. The speaker is identified and Joseph includes a note on each person's occupation, age or achievements. Both his questions and the subject's reply are printed.

340 Joy, Carol M., and Terry Ann Mood. **Colorado Local History: A Directory.** Denver: Colorado Library Association, 1975. ED 114 318. In this directory "oral history" is a cross reference. The user must look under the subject heading "interviews." Information is minimal.

341 Joyner, Charles W. "Oral History as a Communicative Event: A Folkloristic Perspective." **Oral History Review** (1979), 47-52. Writing as a folklorist, Joyner believes "oral history should be used in conjunction with other methods of historical inquiry." He makes a distinction between facts and the truth.

342 Juarez, Rolando A. "What the Tape Recorder Has Created: A Broadly-based Exploration into Contemporary Oral History Practice." **Aztlan** 7 (Spring 1976), 99-118. Juarez defines oral history; gives a sketch of how projects are carried out; and a brief listing of current and past work, citing standard authors in the field. He contrasts the historical method with that of the social scientist. He believes oral history material is of value to social science.

343 Juhnke, James C. "The Victories of Nonresistance: Mennonite Oral Tradition and World War I." **Fides et Historia** 7 (Fall 1974), 19-25.

_____, see also Sprunger, Keith L.

344 "'Just a Young Fella Comin' Thru the Country': Oral History from the Texas Frontier." **American West** 16 (January/February 1979), 14-17, 59. The transcription of the reminiscences of Mabel Aiken Bayer (1898-1978), a native of Granbury, as told to Jan Stopschinski.

345 Kachaturoff, Grace, and Frances Greenebaum. "Oral History in the Social Studies Classroom." **Social Studies** 72 (January/February 1981), 18-22. The authors see oral history as a method to be used to combat a lack of interest in social studies and make history live for students. By concentrating on older members of their families, children can close the generation gap and better understand how national events, e.g., the New Deal, affected people close to them.

346 Kahn, Kathy. **Fruits of Our Labor.** New York: Putnam, 1982. Kahn's book is based on interviews with American and Soviet workers. Its costs were jointly underwritten by the National Endowment for the Humanities and Novosti Books, a Russian state publishing house. The background information on her subjects is lengthier than in most books of this type and includes the transla-

tor's notes on the nuances of language. In both countries she concentrated on workers in traditional occupations, branching out briefly for an interview with a reindeer herder.

347 _____. **Hillbilly Women.** New York: Doubleday, 1972. Women in the Appalachian Mountains and the migrant ghettos of the North recorded interviews with Kahn. Each speaker had the opportunity to make changes after the tape was transcribed and edited. The women are identified and Kahn provides explanatory material with each narrative. Circumstances afforded few opportunities for formal education but several are songwriters and all are eloquent. The appendix has descriptions of Appalachian grassroots organizations and publications with addresses.

348 Kann, Kenneth. "Reconstructing the History of a Community." **International Journal of Oral History** 2 (February 1981), 4-12. Jewish immigrants who came to Petaluma, California, and worked as chicken farmers were interviewed. Contrasts in aspirations and attitudes between them and the children born to them in this country are examined.

349 Kantrowitz, Barbara. "Aged Talk Up the Past." **New York Times** December 18, 1977, Section 22, p.1. The article describes an oral history project called Seniors Remember in New Rochelle, N.Y.

350 Kaplan, Charles D. "Addict-life Stories: An Exploration of the Methodological Grounds for the Study of Social Problems." **International Journal of Oral History** 3 (June 1982), 114-128. Kaplan used oral history to examine the lives of two drug addicts. He discusses how the method illustrates social problems.

Kauroma, Patricia A., see Mamiya, Lawrence H.

Kelly, Jim, see Fraser, Ronald.

351 Kenney, Anne R. "Retrospective and Current Oral History Projects: A Comparison." **Midwestern Archive** 6, #1 (1981), 47-58. Kenney compares interviews with women who took part in the 1930's St. Louis garment industry strike with those done in 1973 with striking teachers. League of Women Voters members of the 1920's are compared to 1977 participants in the International Woman's Year.

352 Kenny, Michael G. "The Relation of Oral History to Social Structure in South Nyanza, Kenya." **Africa: Journal of the International African Institute** 47 (1977), 276-287.

353 Key, Betty McKeever. **Maryland Manual of Oral History.**
Baltimore: Library of the Maryland Historical Society,
Oral History Office, 1979. Reviewed: **Maryland History
Magazine** 74 (Winter 1979), 374.

354 _____. "Oral History in Maryland." **Maryland History
Magazine** 70 (Winter 1975), 379-384. The author,
director of the state historical society's oral history
office, gives an overview of its work.

355 _____. "Oral History in the Library." **Catholic Library
World** 49 (April 1978), 380-384. Key cites four ways
of acquiring material: through routine acquisitions;
buying commercially offered transcripts; accepting
locally-produced tapes; and becoming the depository
for a particular project. She considers how to evaluate
and handle each type. References, bibliography.

356 _____. "Publishing Oral History: Observations and
Objections." **Oral History Review** 10 (1982), 33-45.
Key posits guidelines for analyzing works of oral
history and recommends some titles as good examples
of the type. She believes those which do not meet
exacting standards can still be enjoyed.

357 _____. "Telling It Like It Was in 1968." **Catholic Library
World** 47 (October 1975), 106-109. Key describes
the McCarthy Historical Project deposited in the
Georgetown University Library. Abigail McCarthy,
wife of 1968 presidential candidate Eugene McCarthy,
was the moving force behind the project. Campaign
workers and supporters were interviewed.

358 Khrushchev, Nikita S. **Khrushchev Remembers.** Introduction, commentary and notes by Edward Crankshaw.
Ed. and trans. Strobe Talbot. Boston: Little, Brown,
1970. A publisher's note vouches for the authenticity
of the material presented here "emanating from various
sources at various times and in various circumstances."
The transcripts of Khrushchev's words were organized
by Talbot into two parts: the first covers his early
career, the 1936 purges, World War II and the events
following Stalin's death; the second deals with the
Korean War, Vietnam, Castro and matters in the
world outside the Soviet Union's borders. Photos and
index.

359 "Khrushchev Tape Is Revealed Here." **New York Times**
March 7, 1974, p.11. Time, Incorporated gives more
Khrushchev tapes to Columbia University and announces
publication of the Little, Brown edition of **Khrushchev
Remembers.**

360 Kielman, Chester V. "The Texas Oil Industry Project."
Wilson Library Bulletin 40 (March 1966), 616-618.
Kielman records the first effort to document a major
American industry which was occasioned by the fiftieth
anniversary of Spindletop, the East Texas gusher.
Between 1952 and 1954 218 interviews were recorded.
Interest in the project was responsible for the Univer-
sity of Texas' receiving several manuscript collections
concerned with the oil industry.

361 King, Michael. "New Zealand Oral History: Some Cultural
and Methodological Considerations." **New Zealand
Journal of History** 12 (1978), 104-123. King did a
biographical study of a Maori princess. He reflects
on the experience of dealing with a native people,
believing he learned lessons applicable in similar
situations.

362 Kinney, J.P. "Beginning Indian Lands Forestry: An Oral
History Interview." **Forest History** 15 (July 1971),
6-15. The interview was conducted in 1960. Kinney
was the first head of the Forestry Branch of the Office
of Indian Affairs in 1910.

363 Kirszner, Laurie Getz. "Mark Twain Recites His Memoirs:
Oral History and Popular Autobiography." Doctoral
dissertation, Temple University, 1976. (Dissertation
Abstracts, 37:2183A). Kirszner believes Twain's **Autobiography** (1924 edition), has been overlooked by
scholars. She treats the work as an oral history transcript and attributes its popular appeal at the time
of publication to its reflective qualities.

364 _____. "Oral History: Up from Obscurity." **Freshman
English News** 7 (Winter 1979), 1-2. Two common problems in student assignments are a lack of interest
in an assigned subject and the shortage of material
on a given topic. Kirszner believes projects centered
on oral history can overcome these obstacles. Her
students take notes rather than taping interviews
with their subjects to foster skills which they will
later use in writing papers.

Knight, Margot H., see Buckendorf, Madeline.

365 Knox, Donald. **The Magic Factory: How MGM Made
"An American in Paris."** New York: Praeger, 1973.
ED 081 050. Knox interviewed production people
and the stars of the hit film musical of 1951 which
won six Academy Awards. Excerpts from the material
are grouped under five topics: preparation, the writing
of the script, filming, music and dance numbers,
and postproduction. Complete cast list and photos.

366 Knudsen, B. "Reminiscences of a Cree Indian: Jimmy Spence." **Moccasin Telegraph** 16 (March 1975), 1-5.

367 Kohl, Herb. "What Was It Like When You Were Young." **Teacher** 96 (March 1979), 14-16, 20. The author, who teaches in Berkeley, California, deals with the problem of doing oral history in the fourth through sixth grades. He lists some interview questions which concentrate on the subject's childhood. Going through a family photo album and talking about the people pictured is a method suggested for these students. The article includes a reprint of Foxfire's Sample Personality Questions.

368 Kornbluh, Joyce L., ed. **Rebel Voices: An I.W.W. Anthology.** Ann Arbor: University of Michigan Press, 1964. This is a selection of material from the Labadie Collection at the University of Michigan gathered since 1911. Biographical material on International Workers of the World and their associates sketches the history of this early union. Songs, trial testimony, speeches, poems and letters from the turn of the century appear here. This is not really oral history but is listed here because it is cited in some bibliographies.

369 Korth, Philip A. "Auto-Lite Strike: Methods and Materials." **Labor History** 16 (Summer 1975), 412-417. The 1934 strike at the Toledo, Ohio, Auto-Lite plant was investigated by the author and his students. Through background reading of the Toledo **Blade** and other sources 2000 names of strike participants were gathered. The recollections of strikers, retired policemen and newspaper writers were taped and the material was edited into a slide/tape presentation. The author observes that his and his students' youth helped rather than hindered the interviewing process. Repositories of the material produced are named.

370 Kranitz-Sanders, Lillian. **Twelve Who Survived: An Oral History of the Jews of Lodz, Poland, 1930-1954.** New York: Irvington Publishers, 1983.

371 Krasean, Thomas K. "Oral History: Voices of the Past." **Library Occurrent** 22 (August 1968), 297, 305. The librarian of the Indiana State Library briefly describes oral history and cites a current project of that institution.

372 Krech, Shepard, III. "The Participation of Maryland Blacks in the Civil War: Perspectives from Oral History." **Ethnohistory** 27 (Winter 1980), 67-78. Krech interviewed Joseph Sutton of Talbot County, Maryland (born 1885) in 1976. After a brief background on the county's history, five passages from the interview are excerpted. They cover recruitment of slaves in the Civil War and the experiences of Sutton's maternal grandfather. The author measures Sutton's remembrances against printed sources for validity.

Kusnerz, Peggy Ann, see #10.

373 Kuuisto, Kathy. "Budgetary Restraint and Oral History." **Canadian Oral History Association Journal** 4, #1 (1979), 1-3. Government funding is falling at a time when collecting oral history for museums and historical preservation projects is coming into its own.

La Clare, Leo, see Clare, Leo La.

374 Lance, David. "Oral History Archives: Perceptions and Practices." **Oral History** 8, #2 (1980), 59-63. Lance sees British oral history moving away from autobiographical works to the study of selected topics.

375 _____. "Oral History in Britain." **Oral History Review** (1974), 64-76. The author recalls the history of the movement, which in Britain began in the 1930's. He describes his work in the Department of Sound Records in the Imperial War Museum at length. A listing of oral history centres in Britain and Ireland with a description of their contents is appended.

376 _____. "Oral History Recording: A Note on Legal Considerations." **Oral History** (1976), 96-97. The director of the Imperial War Museum provided a short description of how the copyrighting of materials is handled by his office.

Langenbach, Randolph, see Harevan, Tamara K.

377 Langlois, William J. **Aural History Institute of British Columbia: Manual.** Victoria, B.C.: The Institute, 1974.

_____, see also Aural History Convention; Provincial Archives of British Columbia.

378 Larson, David R. "Oral History in Ohio." **Ohio History** 78 (Winter 1969), 49-52. Larson describes a project conducted by the Ohio Historical Society aimed at supplementing written material in which the institution specializes. The program is collecting information for two topics, the Distinguished Ohioans Series and Recent Ohio Political History. Funding is expected to come from private grants.

379 Lawrence, Ken. "Oral History of Slavery." **Southern Exposure** 1 (Winter 1974), 84-86. The author claims that the techniques of oral history "were originally developed and refined in the late 1920's at Southern University and Fisk University" in work with former slaves. The concept was then extended by the WPA Writers' Projects. Lawrence cites several publications based on the universities' work. The article contains two excerpts from ex-slave interviews.

380 Lazzell, Ruleen. "Life on a Homestead: Memories of Minnie A. Crisp." **New Mexico Historical Review** 54 (January 1979), 59-64. Excerpts from an interview with Mrs. Crisp are bridged by Lazzell's narrative material.

381 Lehane, Stephen, and Richard Goldman. "Oral History: Research and Teaching Tool for Educators." **Elementary School Journal** 77 (January 1977), 173-181. The authors summarize six studies they conducted. Their Kent State Study, which was concerned with the National Guard shootings in 1970, is described in detail. 25 references.

382 Lesy, Michael. **Time Frames: The Meaning of Family Pictures.** New York: Random House, 1980. Though cited by some as oral history, this title does not truly qualify. The names are pseudonymous and the pictures unidentified. Educated as an historian, Lesy couples history and photography.

383 Leuthner, Stuart. **The Railroaders.** New York: Random House, 1983. Reviewed: **Wall Street Journal** November 14, 1983, p.24; **Library Journal** 108 (October 1, 1983), 1873.

384 Levene, Bruce, et al. **Mendocino County Remembered: An Oral History.** Ukiah, Calif.: Mendocino County Historical Society, 1977.

385 Levy, Myrna. "Memories of Memorial—A Study of Oral History." **Orbit** 12 (December 1981), 16-18. Levy describes a project carried out to commemorate the sixtieth anniversary of the Junior School in York, England. The principal had been a pupil there. Excerpts from his interview are included.

386 Lewin, Rhoda Greene. "Some New Perspectives on the Jewish Immigrant Experience in Minneapolis: An Experiment in Oral History." Doctoral dissertation, University of Minnesota, 1978. (Dissertation Abstracts 39:3778-3779A). Seventeen East European Jews who reached the U.S. in the period from 1900 to 1924 were the subjects of Lewin's study. Her findings often conflict with accepted beliefs about Jewish immigrants.

The methodology is discussed and suggestions are made for future work.

387 Lewis, Oscar. **The Children of Sanchez: Autobiography of a Mexican Family.** New York: Random House, 1961. Anthropologist Lewis transcribes the story of the pseudonymous Sanchez family and their life in a slum tenement in Mexico City. Interviews have been "selected, arranged and organized...into coherent life stories." A father and his four adult children are profiled. A twenty page introduction provides background information, discusses methodology and sets the stage.

388 _____. **A Death in the Sanchez Family.** New York: Random House, 1969. This is an oral history of the death of Guadalupe, the maternal aunt of the Sanchez children. Three chapters recount the death, the wake and the burial. Manuel, Roberto and Consuelo relate these events from their own perspectives, telling Lewis how Guadalupe figured in their earlier lives. The material was taped in Spanish and translated.

389 _____. **Five Families: Mexican Case Studies in the Culture of Poverty.** Foreword by Oliver La Farge. New York: Basic Books, 1959. One family lives in a village, the others in urban settings. Each is presented in a separate chapter with narrative material connecting the speech of the family members. In the opening chapter titled "The Setting," Lewis points up the lack of material on poor families in Mexico (c. 1959). Each family is presented as going about its business on a typical day. Conversations were put on paper in shorthand by an assistant. The Sanchez family which is presented here are also the protagonists in two of Lewis's other works.

390 _____. **Pedro Martinez: A Mexican Peasant and His Family.** New York: Random House, 1964. The story of this rural Mexican family was recorded over a period of twenty years by Lewis. Pedro Martinez, his wife Esperanza and their oldest son Felipe each have their say. Born in 1889, Pedro lived through the 1910 Revolution and converted from Catholicism to Seventh Day Adventism. An introduction and appendices on the village, family finances and other family members round out the picture.

391 _____. **La Vida: A Puerto Rican Family in the Culture of Poverty—San Juan and New York.** New York: Random House, 1965. This is a study of the pseudonymous

Rios family. The mother lives with a husband in Puerto
Rico while two of her adult children reside in New
York City. In a lengthy introduction Lewis details
the methodology of the larger study of which these
oral histories are a part. He discusses the poor of
Mexico, touching on language, life styles, states of
mind, and "the culture of poverty," and contrasts
them with the lower classes of Puerto Rico.

392 _____, Ruth M. Lewis, and Susan M. Rigdon. **Four
Men: Living the Revolution: An Oral History of Contemporary Cuba.** Urbana: University of Illinois Press,
1970. A foreword by Ruth Lewis outlines the inception
of this project at Castro's request, the difficulties
encountered and its abrupt end. The four men whose
histories are transcribed here are all of the lower
classes.

393 _____, _____, and _____. **Four Women: Living
the Revolution: An Oral History of Contemporary
Cuba.** Urbana: University of Illinois Press, 1980. Three
white women and a mulatto, representing a cross-
section of backgrounds, were interviewed. The introduction, which deals with the status of women in
Cuba, gives a good overview of women's role in the
revolution.

394 _____, _____, and _____. **Neighbors: Living
the Revolution: An Oral History of Contemporary
Cuba.** Urbana: University of Illinois, 1978. The subjects of this book are members of five unrelated
families who live in a Havana suburb. The research
was conducted from March, 1969 to late June, 1970.
The participants spoke in Spanish and the material
was transcribed and translated. Introductions to each
section provide historical background. A lengthy
afterword summarizes the findings of the editors.
Appendices discuss rationing and household expenses.
Glossary; bibliography of Spanish and English books
and articles.

395 Libbey, David. "Oral History in Connecticut Public
Libraries." **Connecticut Libraries** 23 (Fall 1981), 32-34.
Libbey gives an overview of projects conducted by
the state library and those in some of the larger towns
and cities. He briefly describes their subject matter
and sources of funding.

Liberty, Mary, see Stands in Timber, John.

396 Liddington, Jill. "Working-class Women in the North
West II." **Oral History** 5 (Autumn 1977), 31-45. Lidding-

ton investigated women in the Lancashire cotton industry, examining their work patterns and participation in trade unions.

397 Lidz, Richard. **Many Kinds of Courage: An Oral History of World War II.** New York: Putnam, 1980. Lidz compiled an oral history of the second war from talks with combat troops and internees in German and Japanese-American prison camps. The identities of some subjects are revealed, others are cloaked in pseudonyms. The author introduces each speaker and fills in the background.

398 Lieber, Joel. "Tape Recorder as Historian." **Saturday Review** 49 (June 11, 1966), 98-99; "The Pause That Instructs." 49 (August 13, 1966), 60-61. Lieber writes a popular overview of oral history. He briefly describes the work done at Columbia University and notes current projects nationwide. In the second reference two letters to the editor from readers deplore Columbia's practice of erasing tapes after they are transcribed.

399 Lindqvist, Sven. "Dig Where You Stand." **Oral History** 7 (Autumn 1979), 24-30. After reading several business histories written with company approval, Lindqvist concluded they presented a one-sided view because there was material from workers. He gave up a projected history of the cement industry to compile a book instructing workers how to write their own histories.

400 Lindsey, J.A. "Why Do You Wait to Get It on Tape?" **Tennessee Librarian** 34 (Spring 1982), 15-19.

401 Lochhead, Richard. "Three Approaches to Oral History: The Journalistic, the Academic, and the Archival." **Canadian Oral History Association Journal** 1 (1975-76), 5-12. Oral history in Canada from 1960 to 1975 are examined from these aspects.

402 Lockley, Fred. **Conversations with Pioneer Women.** Eugene, Ore.: Rainy Day Press, 1981. Lockley was a pioneer Oregon newspaperman who came to the state in the late 1890's. He interviewed a variety of the state's pioneers. This book was compiled from talks centering on pioneer women and their experiences. Short biographical introductions accompany some of the interviews. Index of names.

403 _____. **Voices of the Oregon Territory: Conversations with Bullwhackers, Muleskinners, Pioneers, Prospectors, '49ers, Indian Fighters, Trappers, Ex-barkeepers, Authors, Preachers, Poets & Near Poets & Sports**

and Conditions of Men. Mike Helm, ed. Eugene, Ore.: Rainy Day Press, 1981. Another transcription of Lockley's interviews.

404 Lovelace, Martin. "John Guy Meets the Dawes: The Investigation of an Oral Historical Tradition." **Canadian Folklore Canadian** 2, #1-2 (1980), 44-53. Oral history in Newfoundland.

405 Lummis, Trevor. "Occupational Community of East Anglian Fisherman: An Historical Dimension Through Oral Evidence." **British Journal of Sociology** 28 (March 1977), 51-74. Lummis, a British sociologist, interviewed fishermen to determine their attitudes toward social structure in the period from 1900 to 1915. He disagrees with the contention of critics that oral history is unreliable because it doesn't use random sample techniques. The evidence for this study was based on sixty interviews conducted between 1974 and 1976. The sessions varied in length from one to five hours.

406 _____. "Structure and Validity in Oral Evidence." **International Journal of Oral History** 2 (June 1981), 109-120. Lummis believes the interviewer's individual technique and the speaker's accuracy of memory contribute to the wide range of quality in the finished product.

407 Lurie, Nancy O., ed. **Mountain Wolf Woman: The Autobiography of a Winnebago Indian.** Ann Arbor: University of Michigan, 1961. With extensive notes supplied by Lurie, Mountain Wolf Woman tells her life story. The Winnebago was Lurie's aunt through adoption. The material for the autobiography was recorded in the English and Winnebago languages. Two versions are presented: a short summary and an expansion which makes up the major part of the text. Photos.

408 Lustig, Theodore. "Corporate Ear." **Public Relations Journal** 33 (July 1977), 20-22. The author worked for American Cyanamid and reports on his research with former company employees. He urges companies to conduct oral history projects with their retirees as a public relations exercise and suggests ways to use the resulting material for the company's benefit.

409 Lutton, Nancy. "The New Guinea Collection: University of Papua New Guinea Library." **Archives and Manuscripts** [Australia] 6, (1975), 113-119. Lutton describes the holdings, a small part of which is oral history material on language and music.

410 Lynd, Alice, and Staughton Lynd. **Rank and File: Personal**

Histories by Working-class Organizers. Boston: Beacon Press, 1973. The Lynds interviewed union members not the organization's officials for this study. Many of their subjects worked in the Chicago area steel industry. The project's participants are named and briefly profiled. About half were active in the union movements of the 1930's, the remainder since World War II.

411 Lynd, Staughton. "Guerrilla History in Gary." **Liberation** 14 (October 1969), 17-20. Lynd points out that while the interviewers of the WPA Writers' Project collected slave narratives they virtually ignored union workers. The American labor movement was in ferment throughout the 1930's while the WPA was busy recording material. Detroit's Wayne State University is interviewing men active in the United Auto Workers union. Two members of the United Steelworkers were taped and Lynd discusses their histories.

412 Lyon, T. Edgar. "Recollections of 'Old Nauvooers': Memories from Oral History." **Brigham Young University Studies** 18 (Winter 1978), 143-150. Lyon quotes from the reminiscences of elderly Mormons on the subject of early church leaders. The material extracted here appears to be heavily edited and it is doubtful that these are unadorned transcripts.

413 McAdoo, Harriette. "Oral History as a Primary Resource in Educational Research." **Journal of Negro Education** 49 (Fall 1980), 414-422. McAdoo focuses on educational research carried out using oral history methods. She discusses its validity and lists guidelines for evaluation. Proper organization of the data obtained is of utmost importance. Transcription must be supported with sufficient funding for users to derive maximum benefit. McAdoo makes suggestions for research into desegregation and busing using oral history.

414 McArdle, Richard E., with Elwood R. Maunder. "Wilderness Politics: Legislation and Forest Service Policy." **Journal of Forest History** 19 (October 1975), 166-179. McArdle interviewed Maunder about the U.S. government's policies.

415 McBane, Margo, and Mary Winegarden. "Labor Pains: An Oral History of California Women Farmworkers." **California History** 58, #2 (1979), 179-181. Faced with the dearth of documentation on the lives of women farmworkers in California, the authors gathered material using oral history methods. The interviews

are available at the Bancroft Library, the University of Michigan and the Fullerton campus of California State University. They record women's experience from the turn of the century to 1979.

416 McComb, David G. "The Oral History of Colorado Project." **Colorado Magazine** 53 (Spring 1976), 187-196. McComb describes a state history project focusing on the "strategic elites" of the state. He reveals how the subjects were selected and questioned and discusses their willingness to participate in the program. The interviewees are named. The subject discussed, restrictions on use and the length of the tape are noted.

417 McCombs, Carol, and Charles H. Busha. "Historical Research and Oral History in Librarianship." In **Library Science Research Reader and Bibliographic Guide**, Charles H. Busha, ed. (Littleton, Col.: Libraries Unlimited, 1981). The authors define oral history and cite several monographs in the second part of this essay. They list the usual pros and cons. 157 references.

418 McCracken, Jane. "The Role of Oral History in Museums." **Canadian Oral History Association Journal** 1 (1975/76), 34-36. McCracken lists ways in which museums can educate the public. She makes specific suggestions about Canadian museums.

419 McCrindle, Jean, and Sheila Rowbotham. **Dutiful Daughters: Women Talk About Their Lives.** Austin: University of Texas Press, 1977. The authors conducted a series of interviews with middle class British women. The domestic side of life, husbands, children and relations with their mothers are the topics. A biographical sketch introduces each woman.

420 McElheny, Victor K. "Henry Wallace Tapes Recall 2 Roles." **New York Times** November 24, 1975, p.24. The article was occasioned by the opening to scholars of 75 hours of tapes by former vice-president Wallace. Dean Albertson did the interviewing in 1950 and 1951.

421 Machado, Manuel, ed. **The Past Remembered: An Oral History of the Potomac Valley.** Missoula: University of Montana Press, 1980.

422 Machart, Norman C. "Doing Oral History in the Elementary Grades." **Social Education** 43 (October 1979), 479-480. The author describes a program for students in grades one to five and lists some guidelines. Carried out under close teacher supervision, it demands clerical aid from parents in typing the transcripts.

423 Machiwanyika, J., and R.E. Reid. trans. "Extracts from 'A History and Customs of the Manyika People.'" **Nada** [Zimbabwe] 11 (1976), 300-308. Excerpts from Machiwanyika's account of relations between white settlers and the Manyika in Africa.

424 McKenzie, James L., and Robert W. Lewis. "'That Rexroth—He'll Argue You Into Anything': An Interview with Kenneth Rexroth." **North Dakota Quarterly** 44 (Summer 1976), 7-33. American poet and critic Rexroth talks about his work.

425 Mackey, Margaret. "Nineteenth Century Tiree Emigrant Communities in Ontario." **Oral History** 9 (Autumn 1981), 49-60. Tiree is the outermost island of the Inner Hebrides. The failure of the potato crop which caused famine in Ireland touched Scotland at the same time. Many of the islanders migrated to Canada and the U.S. Mackey examines their settlements in Ontario.

426 McLaughlin, Doris B. "Putting Michigan Back to Work: Bill Haber Remembers." **Michigan History** 66 (January-February 1982), 30-35. This excerpt is from a transcript in the Haber Oral History Project. It concerns his work with the WPA in the 1930's.

427 MacLeod, Dawn. "Scenes of the Near Past: Born in the Stone." **Blackwood's Magazine** [Great Britain] 327, #1976 (1980), 430-441. Excerpts from conversations with George Swinford, a Cotswold stonemason.

McMahan, Eva M., see Clark, E. Culpepper.

428 MacMaster, Richard K. "Oral History Speaks for the Other America." **America** 128 (May 5, 1973), 411-413. McMaster describes three projects in North Carolina, Mississippi and Kentucky. Their aim is to record the history of the "ungreat."

McMullin, Ruth, see Meckler, Alan M.

428a McNulty, Anne, and Hilary Troop, compilers. **Directory of British Oral History Collections.** Colchester: Oral History Society, 1981. A catalog of collections in the British Isles published serially.

429 Madden, Charlotte. "Alice Lloyd College Oral History." **Kentucky Library Association Bulletin** 40 (Fall 1976), 3-5. Madden is library director at Alice Lloyd College. She describes the oral history collection, noting that photos make up a large portion of the material.

430 Maglin, Nan Bauer. "'Full of Memories': Teaching Matrilineage." **College English** 40 (April 1979), 889-898. The author touches briefly on oral history in recounting a unit she taught on women's literature.

431 Mahon, John K., ed. **Indians of the Lower South: Past and Present. Proceedings of the Gulf Coast History and Humanities Conference.** Pensacola, Fla.: Gulf Coast History and Humanities Conference, 1975. ED 138 411. One paper in the proceedings deals with an oral history program on Southeastern Indians at the University of Florida.

432 Mahoney, James. "Hearing the Past." **Today's Education: Social Studies Edition** 71 (February-March 1982), 60-62. Mahoney's eighth graders published a history of their town based on interviews with residents. He makes suggestions for similar projects, noting the community's relationship with the school improved following the project.

433 Main, John R. "Publication and Copyright of Oral History Materials: The OISE Experience." **Canadian Oral History Association Journal** 1 (1975/76), 37-41. The Oral Institute for Studies in Education members have ideas about possibilities for new projects and discuss some of the copyright problems they present.

434 "Major Black Oral History Programs." In **Handbook of Black Librarianship** (Littleton, Col.: Libraries Unlimited, 1977), p. 253-257. This is a listing by depository with the address and information about staffing and budget. Each description: cites the purpose of the collection; characterizes the holdings; names blacks who figure prominently in the tapes; and gives bibliographic information on published material.

435 Mamiya, Lawrence H., and Patricia A. Kaurouma. "You Never Hear About Their Struggles: Black Oral History in Poughkeepsie, New York." **Afro-American New York Life and History** 4 (July 1980), 55-70. Black life in Poughkeepsie from 1880 to 1980 is discussed: labor, racial discrimination, the Ku Klux Klan; and the role of churches and social organizations.

436 Mantell, W. **A Study in Oral History.** Knoxville: University of Tennessee Press, 1970.

437 Martin, Charles E. "Head of Hollybush: Reconstructing Material Culture Through Oral History." **Pioneer America** 13 (March 1981), 3-16. Martin set out "to reconstruct the architectural history" of a community in Knott County, Kentucky. He supplemented written records and architectural plans with interviews of former inhabitants and their survivors. He concluded that oral history was a valuable resource in the study of material culture.

438 Martin, Lois. "Oral History—How to Mesh the Process and the Substance in U.S. History." **Social Studies** 63 (December 1972), 322-326. The author suggests using the 1930's Depression as a project for students. She believes some hypotheses should be formed before the interviews take place. Questions should be designed to elicit support for the student's conjectures.

439 Martin, Patricia P. **Images and Conversations: Mexican Americans Recall a Southwestern Past.** Tucson: University of Arizona Press, 1983. Thirteen Chicanos who live in the area around Tucson talk about their lives. Martin does not describe her methodology but has presumably edited the material for a pleasing effect. Photos of the subjects, their homes and surroundings.

440 Martinez, Oscar J. "Chicano Oral History: Status and Prospects." **Aztlan** 9 (Spring/Fall 1978), 119-131. Martinez discusses the current state of affairs in Chicano oral history, points out some research opportunities and lists American programs containing Chicano material. Projects conducted by individuals and institutions are appended.

441 Mason, Alan S., and Gerald D. Saxon. "The Dallas Mayors Oral History and Records Project: A Program of Institutional Cooperation." **American Archivist** 45 (Fall 1982), 472-474. A project conducted jointly by East Texas State University and the Dallas Public Library in 1980-81 is outlined here. Each institution's responsibilities are listed along with the subjects covered in the interviews.

442 Mason, David T., and Elwood R. Maunder. "Memoirs of a Forester: Excerpts from Oral History Interviews with David T. Mason." **Forest History** 10 (January 1967), 6-12, 29-35; 13 (April-July 1969), 28-39. Transcript excerpts.

Mason, Elizabeth B., see Columbia University. Oral History Research Office.

443 Massey, Ellen Gray, ed. **Bittersweet Country.** New York: Anchor/Doubleday, 1978. An example of cultural journalism on the Foxfire model, this collection emanates from the Missouri Ozarks. The separate spheres of man's work and woman's work are covered, along with courting, marriage, "ketchin' babies," crafts and music. Photos, recipes and square dance calls.

444 Maunder, Elwood R. **James Greeley McGowin, South Alabama Lumberman.** Santa Cruz, Calif.: Forest History Society, 1977. McGowin's three sons talked

with Maunder about their father and the family business. Their lumber company was a pioneer in tree
farming. The interviews paint a panoramic picture
of small town Southern life.

445 _____. **Twentieth Century Businessman: An Oral
History Interview with Walter Samuel Johnson.** Santa
Cruz, Calif.: Forest History Society, 1974. Johnson
was involved in the lumber industry in California.
Reviewed: **Pacific Northwest Quarterly** 69 (January
1978), 36; **Business History Review** 50 (Summer 1976),
237-238.

_____, see also McArdle, Richard E.; Mason, David
T.

446 Maurer, Harry. **Not Working: An Oral History of the
Unemployed.** New York: Holt, Rinehart and Winston,
1979. The interviews are arranged by topic: getting
fired; looking for work; supplementing unemployment
compensation, legally and otherwise. Separate chapters
deal with the older worker and minority youth. Maurer
uses pseudonyms throughout. He believes the U.S.
unemployment rate is double the official government
statistic. His introduction makes points about unemployment picture of 1979 which are still valid for
the economy of the early 1980's. The scene of each
interview is set with a short biographical note. Maurer's
questions precede his subject's answers.

447 Maynard, John. "Community Writing." **Local Historian**
[Great Britain] 13 (February 1979), 276-280. The
author discusses examples of printed memoirs in
Britain, comparing the tales with happenings and
attitudes of his own childhood. Brief bibliography.

448 Mazuzan, George T. "In Search of the Recent Past:
The Eighth Annual Colloquium of Oral History Association." **Oral History Review** (1974), 77-91. Mazuzan
describes most of the talks presented at the 8th Colloquium.

449 _____, and Gerald Twomey. "Oral History in the
Classroom." **Social Studies** 68 (January-February
1977), 14-19. The authors define oral history and
discuss the role of the interviewer. Intelligence, sensi-
tivity and thorough preparation are indispensable
to the oral historian. They suggest ways to obtain
the maximum amount of material from each interview.
They recommend classroom projects centering on
students' family history.

450 Meckler, Alan M., and Ruth McMullin. **Oral History**

Collections. New York: Bowker, 1975. This catalog of collections in libraries, oral history centers and archives is arranged in two parts: a name-subject index; and a listing by state of American centers. Collections in Canada, the United Kingdom and Israel make up an eight page addendum. Information in the name-subject index is minimal, often only citing the collection which contains material on the desired person or subject. The centers section lists each collection by name and address; gives a description of the program and its purpose; and takes note of restrictions on use.

451 Medicine, Beatrice. "Oral History as Truth: Validity in Recent Court Cases Involving Native Americans." In **Trends and New Vistas in Contemporary Native American Folklore Study**, Stephen Mannenbach, ed. (Bloomington: Indiana Folklore Forum, 1976), p.1-5. (Bibliographic and Special Series, No. 15). Medicine here calls "oral tradition" oral history citing its use in the 'Consolidated Wounded Knee Cases.' The occupation of Wounded Knee in 1973 by members of the American Indian Movement resulted in court proceedings which delved into the history of nineteenth century Indian treaties.

452 Medved, Michael, and David Wallechinsky. **What Really Happened to the Class of '65?** New York: Random House, 1976. The authors were members of the Palisades High School (Los Angeles, Calif.) class of 1965 which was featured in a **Time Magazine** cover story on "Today's Teenagers." Ten years after graduation they interviewed some of their classmates on the subject of life after high school. The opening chapter relates some of the interviewees reactions on hearing the news of the John Kennedy's assassination. Each subsequent chapter is devoted to one person, containing a transcript of his interview and others' opinions of his personality and actions. The authors describe their classmates as they appear at the time of the interview. Photos from the yearbook are paired with a current snapshot. Readers will laugh and cringe in remembrance of their own high school years.

453 Mehaffy, George L., and Thad Sitton. "Oral History: A Strategy That Works." **Social Education** 41 (May 1977), 378-381. The authors recommend oral history as a way to bridge the distance between subjects (e.g., history and social sciences) and involve students

in the life of their own communities. They see oral history as a way to generate enthusiasm for learning because the interviews produce something tangible. Suggestions for projects and short bibliography.

454 _____, _____, and O.L. Davis, Jr. **Oral History in the Classroom**. Washington, D.C.: National Council for the Social Studies, 1979.

455 _____, and _____. "Oral History Tells Its Own Story: The Loblolly Project." **Social Studies** 68 (November/December 1977), 231-235. The article reports on a project in Gary, Texas and contains a transcript by a former student.
_____, see also 642a.

456 Meir, Golda. **A Land of Our Own: An Oral Autobiography.** Marie Syrkin, ed. New York: Putnam, 1973. Not a life history in the accepted sense, this is a collection of Meir's oral statements. It includes excerpts from interviews, talks before various groups, trial testimony, and speeches to the United Nations and the Knesset. Index.

457 Mellon, Knox. "Oral History, Public History and Historic Preservation: California Birds of a Feather." **Oral History Review** 9 (1981), 85-95. Mellon discusses his experiences in California with neighborhood preservation and gentrification.

458 _____. **Training and Techniques of Oral History. Final Report**. Washington, D.C.: Office of Education, 1971. ED 065 369. Through an investigation of working women in Southern California, undergraduates were introduced to a variety of oral history techniques. The project sought to develop a curriculum guide for training liberal arts majors in methods of historical research.

459 Meltzer, Milton. "Using Oral History: A Biographer's Point of View." **Oral History Review** (1979), 42-46. Meltzer used interview tapes made by the Bancroft's Regional Oral History Office in his research for a biography of photographer Dorothea Lange. The collection also contained tapes made by Lange's husband. A two page comment by Suzanne Riess, a ROHO interviewer, is appended.

460 Menninger, Robert. "Some Psychological Factors Involved in Oral History Interviewing." **Oral History Review** (1975), 68-75. The author thinks most people derive satisfaction from being interviewed and that this enhances the resultant material. Subjects who refuse

to answer questions on certain topics should not be pressed. The interviewer would do well to pursue another line of inquiry.

461 Meredith, H.L., and V.E. Milam. "Cherokee Vision of 'Eloh.'" **Indian History** 8 (Winter 1975), 19-23.

462 Meyer, Eugenia, and Alicia Olivera De Bonfil. "Oral History in Mexico." **Journal of Library History** 7 (October 1972), 360-365. The authors describe the Archivo Sonoro, a Mexican oral history program, which originally concentrated on the history of the Mexican Revolution of 1910. The most valuable interviews are published in an ongoing series of booklets. Now housed in the Museum of Anthropology, its scope has been expanded to study rural education, the Mexican movie industry and national politics.

Meyer, John R., see Allen, Rodney F.

Michael, Douglas O., see Deekle, Peter V.

463 Michel, Sonya. "Family and Community Networks Among Rhode Island Jews: A Study Based on Oral Histories." **Rhode Island Jewish History Notes** 7 (November 1978), 513-533.

Milam, V.E., see Meredith, H.L.

464 Miller, Donald E., and Lorna Touryan Miller. "Armenian Survivors: A Typological Analysis of Victim Response." **Oral History Review** 10 (1982), 47-72. Students in Armenian studies at UCLA and others gathered oral history material on the 1915 massacre. The Millers examine six typical responses to the killings.

465 Miller, Lynn F., and Sally S. Swenson. **Lives and Works: Talks with Women Artists.** Metuchen, N.J.: Scarecrow Press, 1981. Swenson interviewed the fifteen women delineated here. Alice Neel, Judith Brodsky, Louise Bourgeois, Nancy Spero, and May Stevens talk about their philosophies of life and art and the mediums in which they work. Each is also profiled in a brief biographical sketch. Photos of the artist and her work.

466 Miller, Merle. **Lyndon: An Oral Biography.** New York: Random House, 1980. Oral recollections of former president Lyndon B. Johnson are interspersed with material from his friends, family, political cronies and opponents. Miller bridges their words with explanatory narrative and arranges the whole in chronological order. A wealth of notes, addenda, bibliography, index and glossary make this a model of completeness.

467 _____. **Plain Speaking: An Oral Biography of Harry**

S Truman. New York: Berkley, 1973. Miller interviewed the former president, his friends, family and others. The book is arranged chronologically. His questions accompany the respondant's answer. Miller accumulated the notes and tapes on which this volume is based for a tv series which was never broadcast. His engaging preface sets the stage and provides a good introduction to the kind of man Truman was and his place in American history.
_____, see also Mitgang, Herbert.

468 Mills, J.C. "Oral History in a Government Agency." **Tennessee Librarian** 34 (Spring 1982), 24-26. Mills discusses the Tennessee Valley Authority.

469 Mintz, Sidney. **Worker in the Cane: A Puerto Rican Life History.** New Haven: Yale University Press, 1960. Material for this book was gathered by Mintz in 1953 and 1956 while he was a graduate student in anthropology. His interview questions are reprinted with the answers of Taso, the sugar cane worker, and his wife Eli. Taso's written statements make up another portion of the book. Glossary and list of other people who play a part in the lives of Taso and his wife.

470 Misztal, Bronislaw. "Autobiographies, Diaries, Life Histories and Oral Histories of Workers as a Source of Socio-Historical Knowledge." **International Journal of Oral History** 2 (November 1981), 181-194. Misztal used these primary sources and examines the difficulties they present to the historian trying to gain objective insights. He lists ways to overcome the problems.

471 Mitchell, David J. "'Living Documents': Oral History and Biography." **Biography** 3 (Fall 1980), 283-296.

472 Mitgang, Herbert. "Publishing: History Via Tape Recorder." **New York Times** August 15, 1980, Section 3, p.20. Mitgang interviewed Merle Miller about **Lyndon,** an oral history of LBJ. Miller met Johnson only once and that in 1940. He did 180 interviews himself and used 276 oral histories in the course of his research. (See no. 466).

473 Mitson, Betty E. "Looking Back in Anguish: Oral History and Japanese-American Evacuation." **Oral History Review** (1974), 24-51. Mitson drew material for this article from the Bancroft Library and the UCLA Research Library. Quotes from a variety of interviews in both collections constitute a large part. Bibliography and extensive notes.

474 _____. "Weyerhaeuser Oral History Seminar: The Businessman Documents His History by Talking with His People." **Journal of Forest History** 19, #3 (1975), 140-142. The seminar outlines Weyerhaeuser's project to document the company history.

475 _____, and Barbara D. Holman. "Red Cedar Shingles & Shakes: The Labor Story. Oral History Interviews with Elwood R. Maunder." **Journal of Forest History** 19 (July 1975), 112-127. Interview transcript concerned with the lumber industry.

476 Montell, William Lynwood. **The Saga of Coe Ridge: A Study in Oral History.** Knoxville: University of Tennessee Press, 1970. Montell gathered the stories of this Kentucky community which was founded by slaves of the Coe family after the Civil War. He presents the story of its life from that era down to 1958 when the inhabitants dispersed. Genealogical charts, bibliography, index, photos.

_____, see also Allen, Barbara.

Mood, Terry Ann, see Joy, Carol M.

477 Morrison, Joan, and Charlotte Fox Zabusky. **American Mosaic: The Immigrant Experience in the Words of Those Who Lived It.** New York: Dutton, 1980. The product of four years' interviewing, the life stories related here are cloaked in pseudonyms. Some exceptions are made for people now well-known in the American press. Three questions were asked of more than 100 immigrants: Why did you come? How? What did you find on arrival? Eighty years of immigration history is encompassed in the book: from a Russian arrival in 1898 to a Johnny-come-lately of 1978. Accounts of life in the old country vie with reactions to America's mores and strangeness.

478 Morrissey, Charles T. "The Case for Oral History." **Vermont History** 31 (July 1963), 145-155. Morrissey discusses the pros and cons of oral history and notes several existing collections on American statesmen which contain mountains of documents. Accounts of events which are preserved on paper can be just as inaccurate as a person's memory. He urges the interviewing of more than one participant in an event to ensure that the truth is recorded.

479 _____. "Evoking the Vermont Experience: Oral History and the Forms of Remembrance." **Vermont History** 49 (Spring 1981), 85-91. In this bibliographic essay Morrissey mentions several oral histories and life

histories whose subjects were native to Vermont or resided there for some part of their lives. Notes contain complete citations.

480 _____. "The Imprint of History on Life-course Research: Oral History and the Berkeley Guidance Study." **International Journal of Oral History** 3 (February 1982), 51-63. The study is an ongoing longitudinal project focusing on children born in 1928 and 1929. Parents were interviewed about their childrearing practices.

481 _____. "On Oral History Interviewing." In **Elite and Specialized Interviewing**, Lewis A. Dexter. (Evanston: Northwestern University Press, 1970), p.109-118. This chapter is reprinted from pages 68-77, **Oral History at Arrowhead.** Morrissey discusses his experiences in talking with political figures as part of his work for the Truman and Kennedy projects. He describes the pitfalls for both interviewer and subject, cautioning against rushing from one topic to the next.

482 _____. "Oral History and Local History: Opportunities for Librarians." **Journal of Library History** 4 (October 1969), 341-346. The author feels there should be more concentration on the "little people" and less on "great men." Traditional historical sources abound in material about the decisions and doings of the great. There is a dearth of evidence to show how common people felt about a particular event or how it affected them personally. Morrissey points out some aspects which are inadequately covered and lists problems he thinks will remedy the situation He urges librarians to get involved in preserving local history.

483 _____. "Oral History and the California Wine Industry: An Essay Review." **Agricultural History** 51 (July 1977), 590-596. The author gives a brief overview of a project conducted by Ruth Teiser, a San Francisco journalist. She conducted 24 interviews with leading California winemakers. The Wine Advisory Board funded the work.

484 _____. "Oral History and the Mythmakers." **Historic Preservation** 16, #6 (1964), 232-237. Morrissey mentions his work in oral history for the Kennedy Presidential Library. He notes how people's memories of an event can become confused with the passing of time. He advocates checking oral material against documents.

485 _____. "Oral History on Campus: Recording Changes in Higher Education." **Dartmouth College Library**

Bulletin 11 (April 1971), 73-80. The author examines several examples of projects conducted to record events on college campuses: student and police confrontations at Columbia University in May, 1968; the deaths of students in Mississippi's Jackson State College. Most university programs focus on distinguished alumni.

486 _____. "Oral History Reliability Is Under Question." **Library Journal** 105 (June 15, 1980), 1350-1351. The author rebuts Oscar Handlin's criticism of the veracity of oral history. He cautions that sometimes too much is expected from interviews. Thorough preparation beforehand is of paramount importance in a successful interview.

487 _____. "Public Historians and Oral History: Problems of Concept and Methods." **Public Historian** 2 (Winter 1980), 22-29. Morrissey discusses how to go about obtaining reliable information.

488 _____. "Rhetoric and Role in Philanthropy: Oral History and the Grant-Making Foundations." **Oral History Review** (1978), 5-19. Morrissey read extensively materials concerning American foundations in preparation for an oral history project on the Ford Foundation. He discusses what he learned, as well as his own experiences with the Ford project.

489 _____. "Truman and the Presidency: Records and Oral Recollections." **American Archivist** 28 (January 1965), 53-61. Morrissey believes that even in these days of the telephone people still make records of conversations. He presses oral historians to determine if written records are available before embarking on a project, especially one centering on a government employee. Interviewers should specialize. Two **caveats:** "...some people know more than they tell and other people tell more than they know."

490 _____. "Why Call It 'Oral History'? Searching for Early Usage of a Generic Term." **Oral History Review** (1980), 20-48. Morrissey recalls early uses of the term prior to Nevins' use of it in the late 1940's.
_____, see also #11.

491 Morthland, John. "The King Remembered (Elvis: An Oral History)." **Country Music** 8 (January/February 1980), 45-55. Excerpts from interviews with people who knew Elvis Presley: his 5th grade teacher, Chet Atkins, record producers and others.

492 Moss, William Warner. "The Future of Oral History."

Oral History Review (1975), 5-15. Moss sees three trends: The "Studs Terkel School"; the growing number of professional historians doing projects; and those using oral history as a component of research for theses and dissertations. He touches on the right of privacy.

493 _____. "Oral History: A New Role for the Library." **Catholic Library World** 47 (October 1975), 118-119. Moss notes the pitfalls of making oral history material available to the public and discusses the monetary drain which a program can inflict on a library budget.

494 _____. "Oral History: An Appreciation." **American Archivist** 40 (October 1977), 429-439. Moss, the chief archivist of the Kennedy Library, attempts to relate oral history to the writing of history and weigh its value as historical evidence. Evaluating oral history is difficult because of the unreliability of the interviewee's memory and the desire, in some subjects, to say what the interviewer wants to hear. The article contains a checklist for evaluating the content and conduct of the interview. Primary evidence and sound analysis are paramount in obtaining documents of lasting historical value.

495 _____. **Oral History Program Manual.** New York: Praeger, 1974. This introductory text for the beginner covers techniques and the processing of interviews. Moss, who was an archivist at the JFK Library at the time of this writing, describes in detail how a major program should be run.

496 _____. "Something of Value." **New Jersey Libraries** 9 (January 1976), 4-7. Moss urges bicentennial projects in honor of U.S. independence and lists 10 commandments for success. The first one is: "Make sure your project is soundly based on a rationally perceived need for information to enrich history."

497 Mozee, Yvonne. "An Interview with Rie Munoz." **Alaska Journal** 4 (Spring 1974), 88-97. The transcript of an interview with the Dutch-born artist. Several of her works are reproduced in color.

498 Myerhoff, Barbara. "Telling One's Story." **Center Magazine** 13 (March 1980), 22-40. This article is based on Myerhoff's book **Number Our Days** (Dutton, 1979) which investigated elderly Jewish immigrants who used an old age center in Venice, California. She believes participants in oral history, especially the "ungreat," take part as an effort to avoid oblivion

after death. Hers was not a true oral history project but the author's observations have implications and lessons for the discipline. Pages 27 to 40 are a discussion by Myerhoff, Roger Abrahams, Jerome Rothenberg, Paul Rabinow and others of questions raised by the article.

499 Myers, C.R. "An Oral History of Psychology in Canada." **Canadian Oral History Association Journal** 1 (1975/76), 30-33. Myers describes the project of the Canadian Psychological Association of 1970-75.

500 **Nations Remembered: An Oral History of the Five Civilized Tribes, 1865-1907.** Selected by Theda Perdue. Westport, Conn.: Greenwood Press, 1980. Library of Congress contents note on the catalog card: "Extracted from Indian-pioneer history, a 112 volume history collected by the Works Progress Administration in conjunction with the University of Oklahoma and the Oklahoma Historical Society." Perdue's work consists of extracts because the historical society stipulated that only portions of a specific interview could be reprinted and that the speaker's identity not be revealed. Seminoles, Cherokees, Creeks, Chickasaws and Choctaws forcibly removed to Oklahoma from the southeastern U.S. were primarily farmers rather than hunters. Separate chapters deal with entertainment, traditions, religion and education. Extensive notes, bibliography, index and photos.

Neihardt, John G., see Black Elk.

501 Nelson, Kathryn J. "Excerpts from Los Testamentos: Hispanic Women Folk Artists of the San Luis Valley, Colorado: Oral History From Eppie Archuleta." **Frontiers** 5, #3 (1980), 34-43. Portions of Nelson's slide/tape program with a weaver and a tapestry embroiderer.

502 Nelson, Murry R., and H. Wells Singleton. "Using Oral History in the Social Studies Classroom." **Clearing House** 49 (October 1975), 89-93; Condensed in **Education Digest** 42 (September 1976), 58-61. The authors suggest oral history as a way to involve students in learning history. Student projects often produce benefits for the surrounding community. As an example, the authors relate the experience of a project with Native Americans in an unnamed western city in 1960.

503 Neuenschwander, John A. **Oral History as a Teaching Approach.** Washington, D.C.: National Education Association, 1976. This pamphlet gives the background of the movement, guidelines for the interview and an example of a project with a release form and a transcript. References and bibliography.

504 _____. **The Practice of Oral History: A Handbook.** Glen Rock, N.J.: Microfilming Corp. of America, 1975. A collection of essays on different aspects of oral history by Joseph H. Cash, Herbert T. Herbert, Stephen R. Ward and Ramon I. Harris. Reviewed: **South Dakota History** 6 (Spring 1976), 232-234.

505 _____. "Remembrance of Things Past: Oral Historians and Long-term Memory." **Oral History Review** (1978), 45-53. The author discusses the reliability of memory, noting that most people frequently recall certain incidents of their lives. He urges thorough preparation for the interview and re-interviewing for a maximum amount of accuracy.

506 Nevins, Allan. "History This Side the Horizon." **Vermont Quarterly** 18 (October 1950), 153-162; Reprinted in **Allan Nevins on History** (New York: Scribner, 1975), p.275-287. Nevins urges readers to look about them for historical incidents. Economic, social and cultural changes occur continually. Collecting records of the present will aid historians in the future.

507 _____. "Oral History: How and Why It Was Born." **Wilson Library Bulletin** 40 (March 1966), 600-601; Reprinted in **Allan Nevins on History**, (New York: Scribner, 1975), p.288-293. Nevins reminisces on the beginnings of oral history at Columbia University. He recounts some notable interviews with famous people.

508 Newby, Howard. "The Dangers of Reminiscence." **Local Historian** [Great Britain] 10 (1973), 334-339. Newby has doubts about the veracity of some subjects. He cites his experience with British agricultural workers, believing that in some cases they said what they thought the interviewer wanted to hear.

509 Newman, Dale. "Culture, Class and Christianity in a Cotton Mill Village." **Oral History** 8 (Autumn 1980), 36-47. Newman examined a North Carolina Piedmont county using oral history techniques to fill gaps in the written historical record. This article is notable for its appendix listing documents, newspapers and census records which he scanned.

510 Newton, Richard F. "Oral History: Using the School as an Historical Institution." **Clearing House** 48 (October 1973), 73-78. Newton proposes that students study their own school as an oral history project, directing and running the program themselves. All segments of the population, including custodial staff and drop-outs, should take part. Material not easily obtained from written sources is the most valuable. The author believes that if students are interested in the content, they will take the trouble to learn how best to deal with its form.

511 Nicolaisen, W.F.H. "English Jack and American Jack." **Midwestern Journal of Language and Folklore** 4 (Spring 1978), 27-36.

512 Niethammer, Lutz. "Oral History In USA." **Archiv Sozial-geschte** 18 (1978), 457-501.

513 North Texas State University. Denton. **Oral History Collection.** Denton, 1972. This catalog of the university's collection is indexed by the name of the inter-viewee. Information under each entry includes a synopsis of the material, the terms of use and the date of the interview.

Novek, Minda, see Rosen-Bayewitz, Passi.

514 Nunis, Doyce B., Jr. "The Library and Oral History." **California Librarian** 22 (July 1961), 139-144. This is one of the earliest articles on oral history. Nunis defines the term and cites several projects.

515 _____, ed. "Recollections of the Early History of Naval Aviation: A Session in Oral History." **Technology and Culture** 4 (Spring 1963), 149-176. Nunis briefly defines oral history in this early article. Talks based on the reminiscences of Garland Fulton and Charles J. McCarthy, naval aviation pioneers, are printed in full. A commentary by John B. Rae notes that while these recollections were presented to an au-dience, their preparation was similar to oral history interviews.

516 Nuschke, Marie Kathern. **White Men Come to Freeman Run: An Oral History of Freeman Run Valley, Potter County, Pennsylvania.** Coudersport, Pa.: Potter Enter-prise, 1976.

517 Oblinger, Carl. **Interviewing the People of Pennsylvania: A Conceptual Guide to Oral History.** Harrisburg: Pennsylvania Historical and Museum Commission, 1978. Oblinger focuses on sociological oral history, examining a specific population in a particular time period. He demonstrates different approaches by using four projects as models and emphasizes the overall concept, not just techniques. List of interview questions, instructions to interviewers and sample senior citizen questionnaire.

518 "Odyssey of a Macedonian Woman Immigrant." **Canadian Ethnic Studies** 9 (1977), 69-76. In this transcript the woman recalls her trip to Toronto to marry a fellow villager.

519 O'Grady, Gerald. "Resources for the Oral History of the Independent American Film at Media Study, Buffalo, N.Y." In **Performing Arts Resources**, Ted Perry, ed. (New York: Drama Book Specialists, 1977), v.3, p.24-31. O'Grady explains the history and background of the Buffalo foundation. There is a brief list of audio, video and related material in its collection.

520 O'Hanlon, Sister Elizabeth. "Sinsinawa Dominican Archives." **Catholic Library World** 51 (July 1979), 26-28. The writer believes oral history should be housed in libraries but not created by them.

521 Okihiro, Gary Y. "Oral History and the Writing of Ethnic History: A Reconnaissance into Method and Theory." **Oral History Review** 9 (1981), 27-46. The author discusses "the writing of history and oral history as method and theory" using his experiences in studies of Africans and Japanese-Americans.

522 Olch, Peter D. "Dirty Mind Never Sleeps and Other Comments on Oral History Movement." **Medical Library Association Bulletin** 59 (July 1971), 438-443. An historical view of the movement and descriptions of some current projects.

523 _____. "Oral History and the Medical Librarian." **Medical Library Association Bulletin** 57 (January 1969), 1-4. The author believes medical librarians should initiate medical projects.

524 _____, and Forrest C. Pogue. **Selections from the Fifth and Sixth National Colloquia on Oral History, Held at Asilomar Conference Grounds, Pacific Grove, California, November 13-16, 1970, and Indiana University, Bloomington, Indiana, October 8-10, 1971.** New York: Oral History Association, 1972. T. Harry Williams gave the major address, entitled "Oral History and the Writing of Biography." Four other speeches concern folklore and oral history. Recent political events, oral history in the ghetto and the Civil Rights Movement are the subjects of other talks.

525 Oliver, Peter. "Oral History: One Historian's View." **Canadian Oral History Association Journal** 1 (1975/76), 13-19. Oliver believes oral history is a good tool for examining social life and popular thought in the twentieth century.

526 Oliver, W.H. "Oral and Other History." **New Zealand Journal of History** 12 (1978), 99-103. Oliver urges checking oral evidence against written sources.

527 Olsen, Germaine L. "Oral History from Four Perspectives." **Journal of Library and Information Science** 5 (October 1979), 151-180; 6 (April 1980), 42-70. Olsen chronicles the growth of the movement, discusses the work of the Oral History Association, cites problems and some solutions to bibliographic control of the material. In the second article she considers problems in the conduct of the interview posed by the interviewer and the subject.

528 Olson, Gayle Clark. "Campus Cop Talk: The Oral Historian, the Law Enforcement Officer, and the War in Isla Vista." **Oral History Review** 10 (1982), 1-31. The Isla Vista neighborhood of Santa Barbara, California, was the site of riots in 1970. Olson's article examines the testimony of the police involved and chronicles the history of their department from 1954 to 1980.

529 Olson, Mary, and Barbara A. Hatcher. "Cultural Journalism: A Bridge to the Past." **Language Arts** 59 (January 1982), 46-50; Condensed in **Education Digest** 47 (May 1982), 46-48. The authors propose classroom projects in the Foxfire mode as a way to involve students and make them aware of the past. The projects can improve their reading, writing, listening and speaking skills. Eighteen tips for a successful unit are listed along with a short bibliography on cultural journalism.

530 "Oral History." **History Workshop** [Great Britain] 8 (1979), i-iii. This unsigned editorial concludes that oral history is a valid method of doing research. The writer mentions several recent historical works which employ its techniques.

531 "Oral History as a Teaching Tool." **Oral History Review** (1973), 29-47. This is the transcript of a panel which took place at the 7th colloquium. Eliot Wigginton and a colleague discussed Foxfire. Other participants were from the University of Maine and Gainesville, Florida.

532 "Oral History Evaluation Guidelines: The Wingspread Conference." **Oral History Review** (1980), 6-19. Program/project guidelines, ethical/legal guidelines, tape/transcript processing guidelines, interview content and conduct guidelines are printed here. Conference bibliography.

533 **Oral History in All 50 States: Two Major Openings, Input/Output, 1975.** New York: Columbia University, Oral History Research Office, 1975. ED 118 055. This booklet summarizes the growth of the movement from 1965 to 1975. The Columbia office opened the archives of material on Francis Perkins and Henry Wallace to researchers. Bibliography of publications which cite or quote material in the university's collections.

534 **An Oral History of Northwestern Colorado.** Carolyn Dirksen, and A. Dudley Gardner, eds. 1981. An historic preservation project carried out by students of Colorado Northwestern Community College.

535 **Oral History: What? Why? How? Guidelines for Oral History.** Harrisburg: Pennsylvania State Dept. of Education, 1975. ED 117 014. The guidelines promulgated in this booklet are aimed at high school students. Nine different teaching units used in the state's schools are described. A list of suggested subjects are included along with tips on interviewing. Nationwide list of publications done by students based on the Foxfire mode.

536 **El Oro y el Futuro del Pueblo: An Oral History and Literature Collection Project.** Rose de Tevis, Margaret Garcia, and Erwin Rivera, eds. Albuquerque, N.M.: De Colores, 1979. Interviews, poems and pictures of Albuquerque's Chicano population by students from eight high schools in the city.

537 Orton, John W. "Oral History and the Genealogical Society." **Catholic Library World** 47 (October 1975), 110-112. Orton describes the work of the Genealogical Society of the Church of Jesus Christ of Latter-Day Saints in recording family pedigrees in the Pacific Islands. Oral History techniques are used to establish lineages in the absence of written records.

538 Ostry, Bernard. "The Illusion of Understanding: Making the Ambiguous Intelligible." **Oral History Review** (1977), 7-16. The author discusses his experiences as an oral historian with Canadian political leaders, Indians and others.

539 _____. "Speech Delivered to the 1976 Oral History Colloquium." **Canadian Oral History Association Journal** 3, #1 (1978), 1-9. Several examples of the use of oral history by academics, amateurs and museum staff in Canada in the period 1930 to the 1970's are described.

540 Otto, John Solomon. "Hard Times Blues (1929-40): Down-home Blues Recordings as Oral Documents." **Oral History Review** (1980), 73-80. Otto examines the lyrics of blues records issued during the Depression as an expression of the life of blacks in that period.

541 _____. "Oral Traditional History in the Southern Highlands." **Appalachian Journal** 9 (Fall 1981), 20-31.

542 Page, Don. "A Visual Dimension to Oral History." **Canadian Oral History Association Journal** 2 (1976/1977), 20-23. Preserving interviews on video tape is suggested by Page to capture the body language and facial expressions of subjects. He describes a project conducted by the Historical Division of the External Affairs Department of Canada which used video taping.

543 Page, Melvin. "Malawians and the Great War: Oral History in Reconstructing Africa's Recent Past." **Oral History Review** (1980), 49-61. Page collected about 180 interviews and 300 questionnaires on the wartime experiences of native African participants. He notes points of agreement and disagreement between his sources and contemporary documents.

544 Pakenham, Thomas. "The Comprehension of Private Cooper." **Oral History** 9 (Autumn 1981), 61-66. Pakenham interviewed Boer War veterans and others whose lives were touched in some way by the conflict. He explains his techniques and reveals that he was emotionally stimulated by the project. He concentrated on enlisted men because no accounts by them exist in the literature on the war.

545 **Past, Present: Recording Life Stories of Older People.** Sara Jenkins, ed. Washington: St. Alban's Parish, 1978.

546 Patrick, Mary. "Indian Urbanization in Dallas: A Second Trail of Tears?" **Oral History Review** (1973), 48-65. The thesis submitted by Patrick to the Baylor University Oral History Program was based on interviews with Indians living in Dallas. She taped interviews with the head of the Bureau of Indian Affairs Dallas Office and with people she contacted through the American Indian Center.

547 Payne, Peggy. "Recording the Civil Rights Roots." **Sepia** 26 (August 1977), 22-27. The Center for Southern Studies at Duke University is involved in a project to chronicle the movements of the 1960's at the grass roots level. Three towns in North Carolina, Chicago housing projects and the Southern Christian Leadership Conference provide some avenues for research. Perdue, Theda, see **Nations Remembered.**

548 Perlis, Vivian. "Ives and Oral History." **Music Library Association Notes** 28 (June 1972), 629-642. Perlis recounts her attempts to gather information on American composer Charles Ives from his friends, fellow musicians and others. She interviewed 57 people and classifies the material under the headings: insurance; family; friends and neighbors; Yale classmates; and music. Each category of tape is discussed separately.

549 Pettus, Louise. "Oral History: A Tool for Teacher Training." **Teaching History: A Journal of Methods** 1 (Fall 1976), 65-69. Pettus describes a project conducted at South Carolina College for Women which, until the 1960's, produced a large portion of the state's teachers. Students in a social studies methods course interviewed older alumnae on their college days.

550 Pfaff, Eugene J., Jr. "Oral History: A New Challenge for Public Libraries." **Wilson Library Bulletin** 54 (May 1980), 568-571. Pfaff describes a model program conducted by a public library. He covers factors to be considered before instituting the project, its scope and the equipment required. Librarians, in his estimation, are qualified to conduct the interviews. Processing of the tapes and a proposal for their dissemination are briefly outlined in the text and notes.

551 Pflug, Warner W., ed. **A Guide to the Archives of Labor History and Urban Affairs.** Detroit: Wayne State University Press, 1974. The Archives, established in 1960, collect papers and oral history interviews on the American labor movement. Pages 139-168 set forth regulations for the use of collected oral history material and list by personal name those who have already been interviewed. Topics covered, the number of pages in each transcript and the date of the interview are noted. Index.

552 Phillips, Harlan B. **Felix Frankfurter Reminisces, Recorded in Talks with Dr. Harlan B. Phillips.** New York: Reynal and Co., 1960. A project of the Columbia University Oral History Research Office, these interviews were conducted in 1953. The material covers Frankfurter's life from his youth and days at Harvard Law School to his appointment to the U.S. Supreme Court in 1939. Questions precede each transcription. Index.

553 Phiri, Kings. "Oral Historical Research in Malawi: A Review of Contemporary Methodology and Projects." **Kalulu** [Zomba] 1 (1976), 68-98.

554 Pocius, Gerald L. "Oral History and the Study of Material Culture." **Material History Bulletin** [Canada] 8 (1979), 65-69. Pocius weighs the reliability of oral sources. He believes the hypotheses developed by traditional historians concerning the artifacts they are studying sometimes unintentionally distort the truth.

555 Pogue, Forrest C. "The George C. Marshall Oral History Project." **Wilson Library Bulletin** 40 (March 1966), 607-608. The project of the George C. Marshall Foundation centers on the World War II American general. It was begun to obtain material for an authorized biography. Three hundred people associated with Marshall were interviewed.

Pollenberg, Richard, see Scandrett, Richard.

556 Portelli, Alessandro. "The Peculiarities of Oral History." **History Workshop** #12 (1981), 96-107. Historian Portelli presents a view from Italy on the legitimacy of oral history as a resource. He points out that many documents were made after a given event and refutes the argument that the years between an occurrence and its discussion in an interview cause distortion.

557 _____. "'The Time of My Life': Functions of Time in Oral History." **International Journal of Oral History** 2 (November 1981), 162-180. People deal with time in different ways. Portelli discusses the reasons for this and how it affects oral history.

558 Powell, Graeme. "Oral History Collections of the National Library of Australia." **Archives and Manuscripts** [Australia] 5 (1974), 137-142. Over the years the library collected a variety of material which falls under the heading oral history. Powell gives some examples and talks about the archive which dates from the 1920's.

559 Princeton University. Library. **A Descriptive Catalogue of the Dulles Oral History Collection: A Series of Memoirs Concerning John Foster Dulles and His Times; Transcribed from Tape-recorded Interviews with the Men and Women Who Knew Him and Worked with Him.** Princeton: The Library, 1967.

560 Proctor, Samuel. "Taping the Indian Past: The University of Florida's Oral History Project." In **Tacachale: Essays on the Indians of Florida and Southeastern Georgia During the Historical Period,** Jerald Milanich and

Samuel Proctor, eds. (Gainesville: University Press of Florida, 1978), p.194-201. The Florida project was one of those originally funded by Doris Duke. Indians in the area south of the Ohio River to Florida and between the Atlantic Ocean and the Mississippi River are included in the university's study. Interviewers who are journalists, archaeologists and anthropoligists, as well as Indians themselves, are employed in collecting material in English and Indian languages.

561 Provincial Archives of British Columbia. Aural History. **A Guide to Aural History Research.** W.J. Langlois, ed. Victoria: Provincial Archives of British Columbia, 1976.

562 Public Archives of Canada. Sound Archives Section. **Inventory of Main Holdings.** Jacques Gagne, compiler. Ottawa: Public Archives, Sound Archives Section, 1979. This catalog of the archives is in English and French.

563 Pugh, Mary J. "Oral History in the Library: Levels of Commitment." **Drexel Library Quarterly** 15 (October 1979), 12-28. Pugh discusses the demands which oral history places on libraries and suggests ways of coping. She identifies for types of programs and the problems they present. Collection, housing, cataloging and policies for use are covered. Programs which are directed by the libraries in which they are housed are dealt with and the costs in time and money are described. Short bibliography.

564 Purkis, Sallie. "Arbury Is Where We Live." **History Today** 33 (June 1983), 29-32. A project conducted by schoolchildren in a Cambridge, England, suburb found links with the past going back to Roman Britain. A post-World War II housing project whose construction the children chronicled led to the unearthing of Roman skeletons.

565 "Railroading on the Gulf Coast: A Conversation with E.A. 'Frog' Smith." **Tampa Bay History** 2 (Fall-Winter 1980), 41-60.

566 Rakove, Milton L. **We Don't Want Nobody Nobody Sent: An Oral History of the Daley Years.** Bloomington: Indiana University Press, 1979. Rakove interviewed more than 30 people who were active in politics during the reign of Hizzonner Richard J. Daley of Chicago. Each speaker provides his own biographical introduction and answers Rakove's specific questions. Women, including protege Jane Byrne; precinct captains,

six men who ran against Daley; and Democrats who opposed him all have their say. The title comes from Abner Mikva's experience with a precinct captain; one had to be sent, i.e., sponsored, by a Daley trustee before the machine listened.

567 Ranger, Terence. "Personal Reminiscence and the Experience of the People in East Central Africa." **Oral History** 6 (Spring 1978), 45-78. The author examines past work done in Africa in documenting the lives of common people and finds few successes. Those which are not manipulative present a romanticized view. Women remain invisible. He nevertheless has high hopes for future research.

Ranney, Judy, see Freiband, Susan J.

568 Raphael, Marc Lee. "Oral History in an Ethnic Community: The Problems and the Promise." **Ohio History** 86 (Autumn 1977), 248-257. The author describes the strengths and weaknesses of oral history with examples from the Columbus Jewish History Project. Successful interviewing is the result of thorough preparation. During the interview the questioner must negotiate a path between rigid structure and chaos. He points out that taped material will not last forever; voices disappear from the tape after several years. He touches on the subject's veracity and describes methods of verifying material from internal evidence and other sources.

569 Rapport, Leonard. "How Valid Are the Federal Writers' Project Life Stories: An Iconoclast Among the True Believers." **Oral History Review** (1979), 6-17; (1980), 89-92. Rapport worked on the WPA project interviewing people about tobacco growing and processing. He maintains that many of the published life stories are fictional, citing two of which he has personal knowledge. In the second reference he sticks to his guns, disagreeing with those who wrote to protest his contention.

570 Rasmussen, Linda, et al. **A Harvest Yet to Reap: A History of Prairie Women.** Toronto, Women's Press, 1976.

571 Read, Daphne. **The Great War and Canadian Society: An Oral History.** Toronto: New Hogtown, 1978. Reviewed: **Canadian Historical Review** 60 (December 1979), 504-505.

572 "Reflections on the Use of Oral History in Baptist Studies." **Baptist History and Heritage** 10 (July 1975),

149-151. Excerpts from a discussion at an oral history workshop between W. Morgan Patterson and Leon McBeth. Both present ideas for supplementing existing written material on Baptist history with oral projects.

573 Reid, David. "Full of Noises." **New Library World** 81 (August 1980), 155-156. In this basic introductory article Reid urges librarians doing oral history to "do it now" before the sources die.

574 Remley, David A. "Crooked Road: Oral History of the Alaska Highway." **Alaska Journal** 4 (Spring 1974), 113-121. Excerpts from 13 interviews the author conducted with people who built the Alaska Highway during World War II. Photos.

Resnik, Henry S., see #688.

575 Reuband, Karl-Heinz. "Oral History: Notes on an Emerging Field in Historical Research." **Historical Social Research** [West Germany] #12 (1979), 18-20. Reuband analyzes the interest in the movement and the methodology involved.

576 Reverby, Susan. "From Aide to Organizer: The Oral History of Lilian Roberts." In **Women of America: A History**, Carol Ruth Berkin, and Mary Beth Norton, eds. (Boston: Houghton Mifflin, 1979), p.289-317. A black hospital worker reflects on her life. She talks about growing up in Chicago in the 1920's, her job, union organizing for the American Federation of State, County and Municipal Employees, and strikes.

577 Reynoldston Research and Studies. **Aural History in B.C. and Oral History in Canada.** Vancouver: 1973.

578 Richardson, J.V. **Alice J. Appell and the Origin and Early Development of Beta Phi Mu: An Oral Interview.** Pittsburgh: University of Pittsburgh, 1982.

579 Riddle, Almeda. **A Singer and Her Songs: Almeda Riddle's Book of Ballads.** Roger D. Abrahams, ed. Baton Rouge: Louisiana State University Press, 1970. This collection of Riddle's ballads (words and music) is interleaved with an oral history of her life and times in Arkansas. She talks about her father's influence on her songs, rural life and the different versions of her songs.

Riess, Suzanne, see Meltzer, Milton.

Rigdon, Susan M., see Lewis, Oscar.

580 "Rite of Passage: The Commission [on Wartime Relocation and Internment of Civilians] Hearings." **Amerasia Journal** 8 (Fall-Winter 1981), 53-105. Written and oral testimony taken in Los Angeles and San Francisco is excerpted here. The speakers are identified.

581 Rizzo, A. Richard. "Interviewing Italian-Americans About Their Life Histories." **Italian Americana** 3 (Autumn 1976), 99-109. Rizzo's introductory article is aimed at the layperson who wants to record a life history. His list of hints includes thoughts on interviewing a person who is not fluent in the interlocutor's language.

582 Roberts, Andrew. "The Use of Oral Sources for African History." **Oral History** 4,#1 (1976), 41-56. Roberts concentrates on Sub-Saharan Africa, pointing out the pitfalls are not confined to language and culture. Oral evidence gathered in the past concentrated on king-lists. More work is needed with the common man.

583 Roberts, Elizabeth. "Oral History and the Local Historian." **Local Historian** [Great Britain] 13 (August 1979), 408-416. Roberts interviewed 95 people in Barrow and Lancaster between 1972 and 1976. She points up how these talks supplement official records, e.g., many operations performed at home are unrecorded in Medical Office of Health statistics. She believes one of the following circumstances is necessary for accurate memory recall: the speaker understands the subject; it is relevant or interesting to him personally; he/she willingly remembers.

584 _____. "Working-class Women in the North West." **Oral History** 5 (Autumn 1977), 7-30. Roberts concentrated on the women in Barrow and Lancaster, England in her research. The towns differed in appearance and economic life.

585 Rockland, Michael A. **By Myself, I'm a Book: An Oral History of the Immigrant Jewish Experience in Pittsburgh.** Waltham, Mass.: American Jewish Historical Society, 1972. Reviewed: **Pennsylvania History** 41 (April 1974), 237-238.

586 Rollins, Alfred B., Jr. **The Oral History Project of the John Fitzgerald Kennedy Library.** Cambridge, Mass.: 1965.

587 _____. "The Voice as History." **Nation** 205 (November 20, 1967), 518-521. Rollins reflects on the shortcomings of oral history as history, the pitfalls of interviewing and the lack of cooperation from those being interviewed. He foresees projects concerned with the common man, better trained oral historians and the use of video tapes as further opportunities for the growth of the movement.

588 Romney, Joseph B. "Legal Considerations in Oral History." **Oral History Review** (1973), 66-76. Romney believes mutual respect between interviewer and subject is the best basis for a trouble-free program. Ownership, use and copyright are discussed in detail. The right of privacy is touched on briefly.

589 _____. "Oral History, Law, and Libraries." **Drexel Library Quarterly** 15 (October 1979), 39-49. Librarians must be aware of legal matters in dealing with oral history material. Romney discusses contracts, libel, copyright and the right of privacy. 28 notes include bibliographical references.

590 Rosen, B. "Aural History Collections: Time for a Decision." **Australian Library Journal** 23 (November 1974), 374-379. Aural history encompasses oral tradition, formal and informal recordings, radio interviews and film soundtracks. Rosen deplores the erasing of tapes and plumps for the establishment of a central aural history facility for Australian material.

591 Rosen-Bayewitz, Passi, and Minda Novek. **Shiloah: Discovering Jewish Identity Through Oral/Folk History: A Source Book.** New York: Institute for Jewish Life, 1976.

592 Rosenberg, Neil, ed. **Folklore and Oral History: Papers from the Second Annual Meeting of the Canadian Aural/Oral History Association, at St. John's, Newfoundland, October 3-5, 1975.** St. John's: Memorial University of Newfoundland, 1978. Five of the papers deal with oral history. Reviewed: **Journal of American Folklore** 93 (April-June 1980), 229-231.

593 Rosengarten, Theodore. **All God's Dangers: The Life of Nate Shaw.** New York: Knopf, 1974. The author went to Alabama to do a study of the Sharecroppers Union and stumbled on Nate Shaw. Subsequent visits produced this oral history of a black tenant farmer, illiterate but capable of sustained narrative which carries the reader along. Shaw's youth and early life, his twelve year imprisonment for union activity and his homecoming are related. This is a landmark publication in the oral history movement, a model of judicious interviewing and editing. See also #741.

594 _____. "Stepping Over Cockleburs: Conversations with Ned Cobb." In **Telling Lives: The Biographer's Art,** Marc Pachter, ed. (Washington, D.C.: New Republic Books, 1979), p.104-131. Rosengarten discusses his venture into the South which resulted in the publica-

tion of **All God's Dangers.** He cites reasons for the
growth of oral testimony: interest in the common
man and his work and life; the ease of using tape
recorders. He talks about his experiences while recording Shaw/Cobb's life history and the reaction of his
subject's children to its publication.
595 Ross, Martha. "Oral History of Maryland Agriculture:
A Voiceless Past, A Challenging Future." **Journal
of the NAL Association** 1, #3 (1976), 47-50. Ross
deplores the shortage of projects dealing with the
history of the state's agriculture in the twentieth
century and makes some suggestions for remedying
the situation.
Rowbotham, Sheila, see McCrindle, Jean.
596 Rubin, Don. "Theatre History and Oral History." **Canadian
Oral History Association Journal** 2 (1976/77), 46-48.
The author describes the Ontario project, conducted
from 1973 to 1975, centering on theatre history and
the special techniques developed for its success.
597 Rumics, Elizabeth. "Oral History: Defining the Term."
Wilson Library Bulletin 40 (March 1966), 602-605.
Rumics discusses the bibliographic control of oral
history tapes and transcripts. She considers how to
make the material accessible to the researcher who
cannot come to the collection.
598 Rundell, Walter, Jr. "Main Trends in U.S. Historiography
Since the New Deal: Research Prospects in Oral History." **Oral History Review** (1976), 35-47. In this bibliographic essay Rundell cites several works on leading
politicians since the 1930's. He sees books on social
problems as another trend and lists titles on addiction,
racism, feminism and education.
599 Ryant, Carl. "Comment: Oral History and Gerontology."
Gerontologist 21 (February 1981), 104-105. Ryant
points out the value of oral history for the health
of elderly participants. Projects can accommodate
older people of differing levels of physical fitness.
Short, standard bibliography.
600 _____. "Oral History and Family History: The Perrys
of Louisville." **Family Heritage** 2 (April 1979), 50-53.
This is Ryant's account of a family history project
conducted by his student at the University of Louisville.
Excerpts from her interview of her parents make
up a large part of the article.
601 _____. "Oral History and Psychohistory." **Journal
of Psychohistory** 8 (Winter 1981), 307-318. The author,

who is codirector of the Oral History Center at the University of Kentucky, looks into the popularity of the movement and sees it as a way to cross the generation gap. He examines oral history in light of Lloyd deMause's process of "fantasy analysis" and urges psychohistorians to use its techniques in their work.

602 _____. "Oral History as Popular Culture." **Journal of Popular Culture** 15 (Spring 1982), 60-62. The author explores oral history as a phenomenon of popular culture, viewing it as a part of the fascination with nostalgia. He urges historians to cooperate with students of popular culture in exchanging insights and attempting to produce a synthesis of the two.

603 Sackreiter, Lucile. "Assessment of the Grant County Oral History Project." **South Dakota Library Bulletin** 57, #4 (Special Edition 1971), 272-274. An outline of the project and a brief appraisal of its impact.

604 Safford, Jeffrey J. "Montana Livestock Industry Through Oral History." **Agricultural History** 49 (January 1975), 105-107. The Montana Historical Society's project, which began by interviewing as many old-time stockmen as could be found, has narrowed its focus and changed emphasis. The program is now fostering local and regional projects which center on the industry's relationship to state politics.

605 Safier, Gwendolyn. **Contemporary American Leaders in Nursing: An Oral History.** New York: McGraw-Hill, 1977. Safier interviewed seventeen pacesetters in American nursing who are educators, researchers and administrators. Her aim was to chronicle the history of nursing since World War II. Women interviewed were chosen on the basis of reputation after correspondence with nursing organizations and schools. She introduces each in a biographical note and transcribes the interview's questions and answers.

606 _____. "'I Sensed the Challenges': Leaders Among Contemporary U.S. Nurses." **Oral History Review** (1975), 30-58. Excerpts of Safier's interviews with leaders in American nursing from World War II and the postwar period. She discusses her methodology and feminist perspective.

607 Salisbury, Harrison K. "The Khrushchev Tapes Provide Rare Archive for Scholarly Research On Contemporary Soviet History." **New York Times** April 28, 1974, p.19. The tapes were made from late 1966 to a few days before Khrushchev's death in 1971. Their authenticity has been verified by voice print analysis. The memoirs were edited by **Time** magazine correspondent Strobe Talbott. **Time** gave the tapes to Columbia University with the stipulation that their use be restricted for the next ten years.

608 Samuel, Raphael. **East End Underworld: Chapters in the Life of Arthur Harding.** London: Routledge and Kegan Paul, 1981. Samuel drew his material from interviews done between 1973 and 1979 with Harding. Relatives, home life, prison life and criminal activity are the topics.

609 _____. "Local History and Oral History." **History Workshop** [Great Britain] 1 (1976), 191-208. The author urges the use of oral history techniques to flesh out and distinguish the history of one locale from another, characterizing the uniqueness of the place and its people.

610 _____, ed. **Village Life and Labour.** London: Routledge and Kegan Paul, 1976. (History Workshop Series). Excerpted interviews are tied together by the editor's narrative illustrating nineteenth century life in rural Britain. Harvesters, the working country girl and quarrymen are dealt with in detail. Notes and subject index.

Sanders, Lillian Kranitz, see Kranitz-Sanders, Lillian.

611 Santoli, Al. **Everything We Had: An Oral History of the Vietnam War by Thirty-three American Soldiers Who Fought It.** New York: Random House, 1981. Two female nurses add their accounts to those of the GIs Santoli interviewed. The stories are told in chronological order of service from December, 1965 to the fall of Saigon in 1975. Lynda Van Devanter, one of the nurses, enlarges her story in **Home Before Morning** (New York: Beaufort Books, 1983).

612 Saretzky, Gary D. "Oral History in American Business Archives." **American Archivist** 44 (Fall 1981), 353-355. Projects concerned with American business were first conducted by universities. Ford Motor Company, Sears and ARCO are interviewing their employees. The chief beneficiary of business archives are the companies themselves; material is usually restricted and unavailable to outsiders.

613 Sargent, James E. "Oral History, Franklin D. Roosevelt, and the New Deal: Some Recollections of Adolf A. Berle, Jr., Lewis W. Douglas, and Raymond Moley."

Oral History Review (1973), 92-109. Sargent quotes from interviews conducted with the three men concerning FDR to illustrate several points about oral history. The speaker's perception of his role vis-à-vis Roosevelt influenced his beliefs.

614 Satterfield, Archie. **The Home Front: An Oral History of the War Years in America, 1941-45.** New York: Playboy Books, 1981. Reared in the oral tradition of the Missouri Ozarks, Satterfield used oral history techniques to tell the story of World War II as seen through the eyes of those who stayed home. Casting a wide net initially, he narrowed his subject matter to selected topics. They include memories of Pearl Harbor, women alone, men at home, rationing, entertainers and the experiences of Japanese internees, black soldiers, and those of German and Italian ancestry. Satterfield ties the interviews together with more commentary than is usually found in oral histories, including lists of popular songs and lines from radio shows of the era.

615 Saxon, Gerald D. "Oral History and the Dallas Public Library." **Texas Library Journal** 58 (Spring 1982), 26-27. An overview of the program run by the library's Archives and Research Center for Texas and Dallas history.

_____, see also Mason, Alan S.

616 Sayre, A. Reasoner. "The Uses of Oral History: A Valuable Technique in Researching and Executing Public Relations Programs." **Public Relations Journal** 27 (February 1971), 27-29. Sayre briefly describes oral history for the novice, citing two projects: a program at Chapman College in Orange, California; and Shumway's study of uranium mining in Utah.

617 Scandrett, Richard, and Richard Pollenberg. "Remembering Calvin Coolidge: An Oral History Memoir." **Vermont History** 40 (Summer 1972), 190-215. Scandrett was interviewed by Pollenberg on his experiences with Coolidge from 1907 to the late 1920's.

618 "Schaap Shop." **Time** 94 (September 19, 1969), 49-50. A review and bibliography of Dick Schaap's sport biographies compiled from athletes' taped "diaries."

Schippers, Donald J., see #12.

619 Schlosser, Sue Ann. "Favorite Childhood Reading: An Audio-Cassette Project." **Show-Me Libraries** 31 (January 1980), 19-23. Elderly patrons in Schlosser's library were interviewed on the subject of their favorite books of childhood.

620 Schmidt, Patricia C. "Oral History." **History News** 29 (January 1974), 21. This article is adapted from another which appeared in **California Historian** in December, 1971. Schmidt describes a program of the San Mateo County (Calif.) Historical Association which is run by volunteers.

621 Schnapper, Dominique. "The French Social Security Oral History Project: Philosophies, Goals, and Methods." **Oral History Review** (1977), 39-47. This is an account of the first oral history project conducted in France. Begun in April, 1975, it serves as a model for subsequent French work.

622 Schneider, William. "Oral History: Or, Keeping Track of What People Say." **Sourdough** 18 (January 1981), 9-10. Schneider is compiling a bibliography of Alaskan oral history projects. The subject headings will be standardized with two other bibliographies of Alaskan material.

623 "Schowalter Oral History Eyewitness Accounts." **Mennonite Life** 30, #3 (1975), 19-25. Portions of tapes made for the Bethel College project on World War I are transcribed.

624 Schroeder, A.E. "Learning from Oral History." **Show-Me Libraries** 32 (January 1981), 5-12. A wide-ranging assessment of the movement with some observations on work in Missouri.

625 Schwarzlose, Richard A. "J-history Students Like Oral Project; Society Gains, Too." **Journalism Educator** 34 (April 1979), 20-23. The Chicago Journalism Oral History Project began in the author's "History of Mass Communications" class as an alternative to a term paper. The Chicago Historical Society is the depository for the material produced. Schwarzlose cites drawbacks of the project but feels on the whole that it is a worthwhile effort.

626 Scobie, Ingrid Winther. "Family and Community History Through Oral History." **Public Historian** 1 (Summer 1979), 29-39. Family and community history did not engage the attention of historians until the 1950's. Nevins' work at Columbia is described.

627 Scofield, Nanette. "Keep Family Memories Alive." **American Home** 79 (December 1976), 54, 56, 66, 72. Scofield recounts her efforts to record her family's history by interviewing relatives.

628 Sellars, Irma. "Oral History c. 1909: Recollections of Dennis Lynch, A Trooper of the 7th Cavalry, 1866-

1881." **Military Collector and Historian** 25 (1973), 69-71. Trooper Lynch recalls service with Custer and the Battle of the Little Big Horn.

629 **The Seventh Day: Soldiers Talk About the Six-Day War, Recorded and Edited by a Group of Young Kibbutz Members.** Abraham Shapira, ed. Henry Near, trans. New York: Scribner, 1970. Speakers are identified and, in a departure from the usual practice, interviewers are named and given a short biographical note. Separate chapters are devoted to the war's beginning, action under fire and the future. Discussions among the speakers are also transcribed. Glossary, map.

630 Shackelford, Laurel, and Bill Weinberg, eds. **Our Appalachia: An Oral History.** New York: Hill and Wang, 1977. The geographic area extends from eastern Kentucky to western North Carolina. The book is a product of the Appalachian Oral History Project based at Alice Lloyd College in Pippa Passes, Kentucky. It is divided into three sections: life early in this century; the struggle between outsiders bent on exploiting the region's resources and the natives; and the problems faced by today's residents. Questions are included with the narrative. Photos and short bibliographies of subjects. Index.

631 Shaughnessey, D.F. "Labor in the Oral History Collection of Columbia University." **Labor History** 1 (Spring 1960), 177-195. Shaughnessey, a research associate at the Columbia office, reports on a project begun in 1956. The article contains excerpts from tapes on the Southern Tenant Farmers' Union and Edward Lahey's recollections of the 1937 General Motors strike. Appended is a six page list of labor leaders with a short description of the type of material on them in the Columbia project.

632 Shockley, Ann Allen. "Oral History: A Research Tool for Black History." **Negro History Bulletin** 41 (January 1978), 787-789. The author, a librarian and director of a project at Fisk University, lists many past and on-going programs devoted to the black experience in America.

633 Shopes, Linda. "The Baltimore Neighborhood Heritage Project: Oral History and Community Involvement." **Radical History Review** 25 (1981), 26-44. Shopes believes neighborhood projects can be successful only if they are tied to existing community organizations and programs. A collection of tapes of themselves

doesn't tell much about the community if speakers are allowed to ramble over too vast a territory when the questions are not specific enough. In the Baltimore project oral history was one facet of a larger whole.

634 Shores, Louis. "Dimensions of Oral History." **Library Journal** 92 (March 1, 1967), 979-983. This article is based on a paper presented at the first National Colloquium on oral history. Shores believes the tapes should be preserved because they are primary source material and urges filming of subjects. Librarians should achieve bibliographic control over audio and film sources when they include interviews of historic persons.

635 _____. "The Library and Society." **Journal of Library History** 9 (July-October 1973), 143-149. Dr. Shores recalls his education at the University of Chicago and his work to improve the quality of reference tools.

Shostak, Marjorie, see #751.

636 Shumway, Gary L. **Oral History in the United States: A Directory.** New York: Oral History Association, 1971. The directory was compiled from questionnaires sent to association members. About 150 collections are listed. Information includes full address, director's names, major topics and purpose of the program, type and amount of material held. Appendices list institutions which do oral history for internal use only and those which have plans to begin programs. Index.

637 _____. **An Oral History Primer.** Salt Lake City, Utah: Primer, 1973. Reviewed: **South Dakota History** 10 (Winter 1979), 70-72.

638 Simmons, Henry E. **Oral History and the Black Studies Program.** n.p., 1968. ED 035 676. An impassioned, well-done plea for the preservation of black history through taping. Simmons urges that tapes be preserved and the transcripts not be sanitized to conform to white standards of correct English usage.

Singleton, H. Wells, see Nelson, Murry R.

639 Sitton, Thad. "Black History From the Community: The Strategies of Field Work." **Journal of Negro Education** 50 (Spring 1981), 171-181. Sitton believes schools with the aid of community volunteers can carry out a project. He describes his involvement with a program in Lockhart, Texas. Written records were made by Anglos and foster myths about the black community which were revealed and corrected by the project.

640 _____. "Oral Life History: From Tape Recorder to Typewriter." **Social Studies** 72 (May/June 1981), 120-126. In this well written article Sitton lists reasons for doing "cultural journalism" projects in the Foxfire mode in the classroom. Creativity and linguistic skills are developed in the interview. Examples of problems which occur in interviewing are described along with suggestions for overcoming them. Editing and transcription methods are covered briefly.

641 _____. "Public Schools and Public History." **Educational Forum** 44 (March 1980), 276-283. Document and photo archives, oral history and cultural journalism projects are ways to preserve community history. Sitton believes the school is ideally suited to carrying out and preserving the material produced in such programs. Notes include bibliographical references and a listing of cultural journalism programs with addresses.

642 _____. "Thinking About 'Foxfire': Implications of the Classroom Oral History Project." **Illinois Schools Journal** 57, #4 (1977-78), 31-39. Sitton recaps the history of the Foxfire projects and considers the lessons it teaches. He believes classroom projects are feasible, produce a tangible product, help students and create a personal past. Current classroom programs are listed by name with addresses.

642a _____, George L. Mehaffy, and O.L. Davis, Jr. **Oral History: A Guide for Teachers (And Others).** Austin: University of Texas Press, 1983. This is probably the best manual yet published on doing oral history in the classroom. After a historical introduction the authors discuss the different types of projects and how they can be tied to various subjects. Technical matters, equipment, transcription, and storage of the finished tapes and transcripts are described in detail. Material gathered can be placed in a community history archive, used to develop curriculum units or published in a Foxfire-type magazine. Lengthy bibliography.

_____, see also Mehaffy, George.

643 Skeels, Jack W. "Oral History Project on the Development of Unionism in the Automobile Industry." **Labor History** 5 (Spring 1964), 209-212. A joint project by the University of Michigan and Wayne State University dealt with United Auto Workers of the 1930's. The mechanics of the project are discussed and there is a short description of the resulting material.

644 Smith, David. "'What Does History Know of Nailbiting?'"

Llafur [Great Britain] 1 (1973), 34-41. Smith examines the labor movement in Wales.

645 Smith, F.B. "Mayhew's Convict." **Victorian Studies** 22 (Summer 1979), 431-448. Smith considers the accuracy of an interview published by Henry Mayhew in his **Morning Chronicle** pieces. The "Statement of a Returned Convict" is appended to the article. Mayhew's work is noticed here because he foreshadowed techniques of today's oral historians.

646 Smith, Robert Eugene. "Case Study of Economic Competition in the Kwilu, Zaire, 1920: Comparison of Oral and Written Data." **Anthropos** 73, #3-4 (1978), 497-514. Part of this article is the transcription of an interview recorded in 1966 by Smith. Printed in Kituba and English in parallel columns, it concerns an incident in the market economy. Smith compares the interview with a letter in French recounting the same incident.

647 Soapes, Thomas F. "The Federal Writers' Project Slave Interviews: Useful Data or Misleading Sources." **Oral History Review** (1977), 33-38. Soapes discusses the 1930's interviews and notes that American historians disagree as to their value, often drawing opposite conclusions from identical material.

648 Society of American Archivists. Committee on Oral History. "Oral History and Archivists: Some Questions to Ask." **American Archivist** 36 (July 1973), 361-365. The committee questions past assumptions and current techniques and management. Personnel, organizations, locating collections of oral history material and interviews dealing with specific people and subject are discussed. Costs of projects, transcripts and record keeping enter into the equation.

649 Socknat, Thomas. "An Example of an Independent Oral History Project: The Canadian Contingent to the Friends Ambulance Unit, China Convoy." **Canadian Oral History Association Journal** 3, #2 (1978), 18-22. Socknat describes the work of a group of Quakers in China during World War II.

650 South Dakota Oral History Project. **The South Dakota Experience: An Oral History Collection of Its People.** Pierre: 1972- . Running to several volumes, this index is arranged by the name of the interviewee. The description includes: restrictions on use; date and place of interview; a list of the subjects treated. Some of the topics are: homesteading; Indians; frontier life; and the Rapid City flood. Index to subjects and counties.

651 Southern Baptist Convention. Historical Commission. **Microfilm Catalogue: Basic Baptist Historical Materials on Microfilm.** Nashville, Tenn.: 1977. Some oral history material is buried in this publication. Exhuming it is difficult because an index is lacking.

652 Southern Methodist University. Oral History Program. **Oral History Collection on the Performing Arts in America.** Dallas: 1981. Part of the DeGolyer Institute for American Studies, the program's goal is "to gather primary source material ... on all branches of the performing arts." Emphasis is on motion pictures and popular music. Production personnel and leading stars are interviewed. The catalog is arranged by name: the main points of the interview are described, the amount of material is listed, as are terms of use, the interviewer's name and the date of the taping. Steve Allen, Pinky Lee, Arthur Fiedler, stripper Marty Kim and stuntman Dean Smith are portrayed in their own words.

653 Spade, Beatrice. "Americans in Vietnam: An Oral History Project." **History Teacher** 8 (February 1975), 183-192. Spade teaches East and Southeast Asian history at Louisiana State University. The article is a report on her students' interviews of American veterans who are Louisiana residents and served in Asia from the 1950's to 1974. Students were taught the techniques of interviewing and tape recorder operation. They were expected to find their own funding. Most failed to prepare themselves adequately by doing the necessary background reading. Tapes are on deposit at the LSU Department of Archives and Manuscripts and are open to researchers.

654 Spillers, David S. "Recording Oral History." **Arkansas Libraries** 36 (September 1979), 16-22. Spillers' article is excellent for its detailed instruction on tape recorder equipment and operation. He cautions the novice about the pitfalls. Several photos.

655 Sprunger, Keith L., and James C. Juhnke. "Mennonite Oral History." **Mennonite Quarterly Review** 54, #3 (1980), 244-247. The authors describe the Bethel College projects, the first of which concentrated on conscientious objectors in World War I. The questionnaire used in those interviews is reproduced.

656 _____, _____, and John D. Waltner. **Voices Against War: A Guide to the Schowalter Oral History Collection on World War I Conscientious Objection.** N. Newton, Kan.: Bethel College, 1973.

657 Sprunk, Larry J. "The North Dakota Oral History Project."
North Dakota History 43 (Spring 1976), 5-100. The
entire issue is devoted to excerpts from interviews
with 17 North Dakotans about their lives and work
in the state. The state historical society conducted
the program. Each speaker is introduced with a short
biographical sketch. Photos.

658 Stands in Timber, John, and Mary Liberty. **Cheyenne
Memories.** New Haven: Yale University Press, 1967.
Liberty transcribed Stands in Timber's tales of Chey-
enne Indian life. From oral tradition there are accounts
of Custer's defeat and the Cheyenne story of creation.
He describes his own life, part of which he spent
making movies dressed like a "Montgomery Ward
Indian."

Stansell, Jan, see #13.

659 Star, Jack. "Years Ago, When I Was Your Age..." **Chicago**
31 (April 1982), 170-175. Clarence Cook recalls his
childhood in Chicago at the turn of the century. William
Rankin tells of his experiences in the 1930's. Both
are transcripts done by Hull House for its Living
History Project.

660 Starr, Louis M. "Oral History: Problems and Prospects."
Advances in Librarianship (1971), 275-304. An introductory article defines oral history and discusses the
movement, its history and answers questions most
asked by novices. Starr has some thoughts on human
memory and its reliability. He looks for continued
growth of the movement.

_____, see also Columbia University. Oral History
Research Office.

661 Stave, Bruce M. **The Making of Urban History: Historiography Through Oral History.** Beverly Hills, Calif.:
Sage Publications, 1977. These interviews, done between 1974 and 1976, were originally published in
the **Journal of Urban History.** Questions and answers
are transcribed; bibliography and notes for each transcript.

Stenberg, Henry G., see #14.

662 Stent, Ronald. "The Internment of His Majesty's Loyal
Enemy Aliens." **Oral History** 9 (Spring 1981), 35-40.
Stent was a Jewish refugee interned on the Isle of
Man early in World War II. He interviewed himself
recently about the experience and found 36 others
who were there also.

663 Stephens, A. Ray. "Oral History and Archives." **Texas**

Libraries 29 (Fall 1967), 203-214. Stephens summarizes reasons for the rise of oral history and notes the variety of current projects throughout the U.S. He touches on the question of preserving tapes **in toto** and on copyright considerations. The article has some details about programs at North Texas State University.

664 Stephenson, Shirley E. "Fawn McKay Brodie: An Oral History Interview." **Dialogue: A Journal of Mormon Thought** 14, #2 (1981), 99-116. In a 1975 interview Brodie talks about Mormonism and her rejection of its tenets in later life; childhood and education; and her studies of Joseph Smith, Thomas Jefferson and Richard Nixon.

665 _____. "Oral History: Today's Approach to the Past." **Catholic Library World** 48 (November 1976), 157-161. The author defines oral history and lists ways of preserving it in the library. She describes legal problems, transcribing, erasing tapes, funding and equipment. References.

666 Stewart, John. "Oral History Is Beyond the Stage of Talking." **New York Times** May 22, 1977, Section 4, p.9. Stewart briefly describes the beginnings of the movement, Nevins' initiation of the Oral History Research Office at Columbia and takes note of some current projects. Problem areas are: the charge that mountains of minutae are being accumulated to no purpose; projects can be very expensive; and checking the interviewee's statements against written sources.

667 Stone, Frank A. **Using Oral History in Educational Studies.** Storrs: World Education Project, U-32, University of Connecticut, 1977. (Multicultural Research Guides Series, no.1).

668 Storm-Clark, Christopher. "The Miners, 1870-1970: A Test Case for Oral History." **Victorian Studies** 15 (September 1971), 49-74. In the absence of written records on the miners of England since 1880, the author urges the use of oral history to illustrate the social and economic aspects of the industry. Portions of interviews with miners are reprinted.

669 _____. "Some Technical Means for Higher Quality: Recordings in Oral History." **Oral History** 6 (Spring 1978), 114-119. The writer suggests two channel or "stereo recording" and use of a Dolby system. He explains impedance matching.

670 Strobel, Margaret. "Doing Oral History as an Outsider." **Frontiers** 2, #2 (1977), 68-72. Strobel worked with

African and Muslim women, studying them in a cross-cultural perspective. She cites problems of linguistics and culture which can be overcome with some effort.

671 Sturino, Franc. "Oral History in Ethnic Studies and Implications for Education." **Canadian Oral History Association Journal** 4, #1 (1979), 14-21. As part of his research for a dissertation Sturino gathered oral testimony from Italian immigrants who came from southern Italy to the U.S. and Canada between 1880 and the 1940's. He makes some observations on the usefulness of oral history in illustrating social history.

672 Stursberg, Peter. "Banquet Speech to the 1976 Canadian Oral History Conference." **Canadian Oral History Association Journal** 2 (1976/77), 6-10. In researching his books on Canadian Prime Minister John Diefenbaker Stursberg conducted many interviews. He talks about the experience.

673 Sullivan, Margaret L. "Into Community Classrooms: Another Use for Oral History." **Oral History Review** (1974), 53-58. The use of oral history projects in secondary schools is urged as a means of involving the students in the community. Sullivan quotes from tapes made in a St. Louis area project.

674 _____, and Irene E. Cortinovis. "Oral History Recorded and Recycled." **Teaching History: A Journal of Methods** 2 (Spring 1977), 28-31. The authors describe a course taught at the University of Missouri-St. Louis which requires students to make two oral interviews with immigrants. They give details of the assignment and suggest ways to overcome the end-of-semester rush when the tapes are turned in. The best ones from each semester are deposited in the university archives.

675 Susskind, Jacob L. "Oral History: A New Name for an Old Way of Learning." **Clearing House** 52 (December 1978), 179-80. A brief description of Susskind's use of oral history in the classroom.

676 Sutherland, John, and Morton Tenzer. "Oral History in Connecticut: The State of the Art." **Connecticut History** #15 (1975), 9-17.

677 Swain, Donald C. "Problems for Practitioners of Oral History." **American Archivist** 28 (January 1965), 63-69. Though happy about the enthusiasm shown toward current projects, Swain believes more attention should be paid to using material already available. Oral history can overcome some obstacles posed by government secrecy restrictions which keep documents

out of the hands of researchers. He cites the lessons
he learned in conducting a project funded by the
National Science Foundation: high costs; brevity
often produces more useful material than in-depth
interviewing; rapport between interviewer and subject
must be established for success; and lesser known
individuals sometimes shed light on events which
more highly placed people ignore.

678 Sweet, Jeffrey, ed. **Something Wonderful Right Away:**
An Oral History of the Second City and the Compass
Players. New York: Avon, 1978. Second City and
the Compass Players are Chicago improvisational
theatre groups whose alumni include comedy stars
of the last two decades. Joan Rivers, Mike Nichols,
Stiller and Meara, Saturday Night Live regular Gilda
Radner, Shelley Berman and Alan Alda were interviewed by Sweet about their training in Chicago.
He transcribes his questions and their answers. Photos,
lists of principals from both groups.

679 Tales From a Dark Continent. Charles Allen, ed. New
York: St. Martin's Press, 1979. "Based on a series
of interviews with British colonial officers in Africa
which was first broadcast on BBC radio in 1979."

680 "Talking About Life in Vermont." **Yankee** 43 (November
1979), 276-77, 279-80, 283, 285-286. Interviews with
three native Vermonters: a violin maker, a horticultu-
rist, and a river boatman.

681 Tamke, Susan S. "Oral History and Popular Culture:
A Method for the Study of the Experience of Culture."
Journal of Popular Culture 11 (Summer 1977), 267-269.
Tamke explores using oral history as a way of learning
how individuals experience culture and examines
the charge that oral history is unscholarly. Defining,
comparing, analyzing and quantifying data doesn't
tell the observer how a person experienced an object
or event. Literary evidence is not inherently superior
or more truthful for being written down. She touches
on the reliance on transcripts rather than tape, believing that the rhythm, timbre and emotion conveyed
by the interviewee's voice are lost.

682 "Taping Company Lore for Posterity." **Nation's Business**
69 (July 1981), 79-80. Dr. Mimi Stein's work as an
independent oral historian is described. She is paid
by business firms to record their history through
interviews with present and former employees.

683 Tate, Michael L. "Through Indian Eyes: Native American

Oral History in the Classroom." **Teaching History: A Journal of Methods** 3, #2 (1978), 73-78. Members of a graduate seminar at the University of Nebraska interviewed Indians on reservations in their state as well as South Dakota. Questions addressed the subjects of the tribes past history, cultural differences and contemporary problems. Tate describes the preparation and methodology of the interviews and some of the problems students encountered.

684 Taylor, Hugh A. "Oral History and Archives: Keynote Speech to the 1976 Canadian Oral History Conference." **Canadian Oral History Association Journal** 2 (1976-77), 1-5. The importance of the Public Archives of Canada for the oral historian is discussed and evaluated.

Tenzer, Morton, see Sutherland, John.

685 Terkel, Studs. "American Dreams: Holding On." **Chicago** 29 (September 1980) 166-173, 182-183. Excerpts from Terkel's **American Dreams: Lost and Found.**

686 _____. **American Dreams: Lost and Found.** New York: Pantheon Books, 1980. Another in Terkel's series, these interviews are visits with the famous and unknown on the theme "living the American dream." Bill Veeck, Ted Turner, Coleman Young and Vine Deloria are among the household names.

687 _____. **Division Street: America.** New York: Pantheon Books, 1967. The first foray into print by Chicago radio personality Terkel is a collection of interviews with a variety of the city's inhabitants. Each speaker's remarks are prefaced with a biographical note. Though there is a Division Street in Chicago Terkel did not limit his interviews to that area. Vietnam, the Bomb, Chicago's new emigrants and its volatile politics are recurring themes.

688 _____. **Hard Times: An Oral History of the Great Depression.** New York: Pantheon Books, 1970. A landmark among oral histories, this book is the prototype of diverse projects on many educational levels. In the introduction, Terkel interviews himself, describing his youth during the Depression in Chicago. The famous and not-so are given equal space: songwriter Yip Harburg; Cesar Chavez; fan girl Sally Rand; congressman Wright Patman; activists Dorothy Day and Saul Alinsky and positive thinker W. Clement Stone. Terkel's questions precede the subject's answers. For a lengthy and perceptive review see Henry S. Resnik's "When America Was Singing 'Buddy, Can

You Spare a Dime?'" **Saturday Review** 53 (April 18, 1970), 27-30.

689 _____. **Talking to Myself: A Memoir of My Times.** New York: Pantheon Books, 1977. This "oral memoir," unlike Terkel's previous books, is all about himself. Cutting from his recent life to his youth, he gives a picture of his work and the people he has known.

690 _____. "Working On **Working:** Five Lives in the Theater." **New York** 11 (May 15, 1978), 34-40. Interviews by Terkel of himself and five theatre people who worked on the Broadway musical which was based on his book. The wardrobe supervisor, a stagehand and three others who work behind the scenes talk about their jobs.

691 _____. **Working: People Talk About What They Do All Day and How They Feel About What They Do.** New York: Pantheon Books, 1972. Over one hundred interviews with people about their jobs make up this volume. Terkel introduces each person and transcribes his questions along with their responses.

692 Terrill, Tom E., and Jerrold D. Hirsch. "Replies to Leonard Rapport's "How Valid Are the Federal Writers' Project Life Stories: An Iconoclast Among True Believers." **Oral History Review** (1980), 81-92. The writers refute Rapport's arguments (q.v.) calling them invalid and inaccurate. They accuse him of misleading readers.

693 _____, and _____. **Such As Us: Southern Voices of the Thirties.** Chapel Hill: University of North Carolina Press, 1978. These oral histories, gathered by the WPA, were chosen because they represent an individual's perspective on events of the '30's. Black and white mill hands and farm people predominate. Interviewers are identified and the place and year are noted. Instructions which were given to interviewers are reproduced in an appendix. A bibliographical essay discusses books and other material in the same vein which readers may want to consult. Index.

694 Tevis, Cheryl. "Woman Interest." **Successful Farming** 80 (September 1982), 10. The National Extension Homemakers Council is gathering oral history tapes with its members to celebrate its fiftieth anniversary.

695 Texas. North Texas State University. Denton. **Oral History Collection.** Denton: 1980. The North Texas State program began by focusing on Texas politics and politicians. It has expanded to five major topics: ex-governors of Texas; legislation; the New Deal;

World War II; and the university's music school. Information under each personal name includes a description of topics covered, date of taping, interviewer's name and the restrictions on use.

696 Thaxton, Ralph. "The Peasants of Yaocun: Memories of Exploitation, Injustice, and Liberation in a Chinese Village." **Journal of Peasant Studies** 9 (October 1981), 3-46. Peasants who lived in Henan province from 1911 to 1949 were interviewed by Thaxton in April, 1980. Pages 3-36 recount the history of the area in this period. In an appendix (pages 37-46), he offers hints on successful interviewing in rural China.

697 These Are Our Lives: As Told by the People and Written by Members of the Federal Writers' Project of the Works Progress Administration in North Carolina, Tennessee, and Georgia. Chapel Hill: University of North Carolina Press, 1939. Reprinted: Norton, 1975. The preface by William T. Couch explains the project. Names of places and persons are changed to mask true identity. "Instructions to Writers" and an outline of the material to be covered in the interview are printed in an appendix. The interviewers' names appear at the end of each life history.

698 "They Were There: Appalachian Oral History." **Appalachia** 7 (October-November 1973), 30-34.

699 Thom, Deborah. "Women at the Woolwich Arsenal 1915-1919." **Oral History** 6 (Autumn 1978), 58-73. These excerpts by Thom are from interviews with women who did munitions work in England during World War I. The rising cost of living and the absence of other work in the area forced them into the difficult and dangerous jobs.

700 Thomas-Hope, Elizabeth. "Hopes and Reality in the West Indian Migration to Britain." **Oral History** 8 (Spring 1980), 35-42. The writer interviewed a random sample of West Indians to examine their hopes and expectations prior to landing in Britain. A second sample gave her information on the realities of life in Britain.

701 Thompson, Enid T. **Local History: A Handbook for the Collection, Preservation, and Use of Local History Materials.** Englewood, Col.: Englewood Public Library, 1975. ED 110 055. The manual is aimed at small and medium-sized public libraries and historical collections. Gathering, organizing and using a wide variety of materials is dealt with in detail. Pages 43 to 47 are a brief introduction to the use of oral history in these settings.

702 Thompson, John. "Oral History in Australia: Some Problems Discussed at the Australian Folklorists' Conference, Sydney, November 17-18, 1973." **Archives and Manuscripts** [Australia] 5 (1974), 143-146. Thompson summarizes talks given at the conference.

703 Thompson, Paul. **The Edwardians: The Remaking of British Society.** Bloomington: Indiana University Press, 1975. Large blocks of the author's narrative are broken up by quotes from tape recorded interviews with people who lived in the Edwardian era. Country and town life are contrasted. Speakers were drawn from the highest to the lowest social classes. Glossary, bibliography, index and photos of the period.

704 _____. "The Humanistic Tradition and Life Histories in Poland." **Oral History** 7 (Spring 1979), 21-25. In a bibliographic essay Thompson lists a number of written life histories and examines their place in popular culture. Some are entries in contests and represent all levels and occupations in Polish society.

705 _____. "The New Oral History in France." **Oral History** 8, #1 (1980), 14-20. An overview of the movement in France with a glance backward at the past and notes on current work.

706 _____, ed. "Oral History and Black History." **Oral History** 8 (Spring 1980), [Special issue]. The entire issue is devoted to blacks in Britain.

707 _____. "Oral History and the Historian." **History Today** 33 (June 1983), 24-28. A good introductory article summarizing the reasons for conducting oral history research. Thompson explains the techniques and illustrates some of the problems which can arise. He cites several examples of recent book-length publications.

708 _____, ed. (with Natasha Burchardt). **Our Common History: The Transformation of Europe.** Atlantic Highlands, N.J.: Humanities Press, 1982. In this diverse collection Thompson gathers the results of the work of twenty European historians. Work, the peasantry, women, the family, and the Italian Resistance are broad topics examined by the investigators.

709 _____. **The Voice of the Past: Oral History.** Oxford: Oxford University Press, 1978. Thompson describes the precursors of the movement, linking it to oral tradition, Mayhew's work in London and the corner-

cutting of Blythe's **Akenfield.** Chapter Three, "The Achievement of Oral History," is a bibliographic essay, with a British emphasis, on published oral histories to 1976. Other chapters cover the interview, weighing evidence, sifting, sorting, and interpretation.

710 Thompson, Thea. **Edwardian Childhoods.** Boston: Routledge and Kegan Paul, 1981. Thompson interviewed five men, four women in Essex from a variety of backgrounds. Biographical notes on each. Photos.

711 Titon, Jeff Todd. "Life Story." **Journal of American Folklore** 93 (July/September 1980), 276-292. Titon distinguishes between life story and life history on which oral historians focus. Life story is a retelling of a person's life in the trappings of fiction with an introduction, rising action and a climax. Its main ingredient is personality and is, therefore, not a truthful, factual account of the subject's life. Oral history is .concerned with factual accuracy and is a series of answers to a series of questions. In life story the listener is sympathetic, encouraging and nondirective. Oral history should be biography, not autobiography.

712 Toney, S.D. "Oral History on the Road: Experience of the Great Depression and the New Deal." **Humanities** 4 (October 1974), 1-2, 5, 8. (Sudoc NF 3.11); condensed in **Education Digest** 40 (March 1975), 36-38.

713 Tonkin, Elizabeth. "Steps to the Redefinition of Oral History: Examples from Africa." **Social History** 7 (October 1982), 329-335. Tonkin reviews past work.

714 Tonks, A. Ronald. "Oral History and Baptist Churches: How to Implement a Program." **Baptist History and Heritage** 10 (July 1975), 142-148. In this introductory article Tonks outlines the steps to take in beginning a program to record the history of a congregation. Necessary knowledge for the novice includes information on interviewing, equipment and transcription. _____, see also, Charlton, Thomas L.

715 Towle, W.W. **The Oral History of James Nunn, a Unique North Carolinian.** Chapel Hill, N. Car.: Chapel Hill Historical Society, 1978.

716 Treleven, Dale E. "Oral History, Audio Technology, and the TAPE System." **International Journal of Oral History** 2 (February 1981), 26-45. A method for processing tapes developed by the State Historical Society of Wisconsin called Timed Access to Pertinent Excerpts (TAPE) is described. The society treats the recording as a primary source not ephemera.

Troop, Hilary, see McNulty, Anne.

717 Tucker, Veronica E. **An Annotated Bibliography of the Fisk University Library's Black Oral History Collection.** Nashville, Tenn.: 1974.

718 Turner, Robert. "The Contribution of Oral Evidence to Labour History." **Oral History** 4 (1976), 23-40. Turner lists some British publications on labor history, noting that historians have gathered much evidence up to the time of this writing. Extensive bibliography of elite and working people's sources.

Tusler, Adelaide, see #12.

Twomey, Gerald, see Mazuzan, George T.

719 University of British Columbia. Library. **Catalogue of Oral History Phonotapes in the University of British Columbia Libraries.** Vancouver: Reynoldston Research and Studies Oral History Programmes, 1973.

720 "The Use of Oral History in Teaching: A Report on the 1974 Survey." **Oral History Review** (1975), 59-67. The Oral History Association's questionnaire garnered an eight per cent response. Results from high schools, colleges and graduate schools are reported separately.

721 Van Deusen, R. "Memories of Childhood at Warner Castle." **University of Rochester Library Bulletin** 29 (Autumn 1975), 70-74.

722 Vincent, G. Robert. "Sound of History, Story of the National Voice Library." **Library Journal** 90 (October 15, 1965), 4282-4290. The National Voice Library at Michigan State University is dedicated to the preservation and dissemination of the spoken word. Vincent, as its curator, gives an account of the development of Edison's "talking machine" and tells how the archive developed.

723 "Voices of History." **Newsweek** 66 (August 23, 1965), 72. The John F. Kennedy Oral History Project is described and several other projects are mentioned.

724 "Voices of Our Time: Oral Histories Correct the Record." **Human Behavior** 7 (May 1978), 51. A popular summary of oral history for the general reader.

725 Wagner, Anton. "The Uses of Oral History in Canadian Theatre History Research." **Canadian Oral History Association Journal** 4, #1 (1979), 10-13. In this review of published research Wagner criticizes the way the authors used oral material. He believes other techniques used in conjunction with oral history produce more accurate studies.

726 Wagner, Sally Roesch. "Oral History as a Biographical Tool." **Frontiers** 2, #2 (1977), 87-92. An interview

with the granddaughter of Matilda Joslyn Gage gave
Wagner a wealth of background information on the
suffragist movement. Gage's temperament was amply
illustrated by her descendant's stories of family life,
thus adding a new dimension to Wagner's biography
of Gage.

727 Wald, Matthew L. "The Modern Memoirist: Family History
on Tape." **New York Times** August 29, 1980, section
2, p.2. Mary C. O'Connell is taping oral autobiography
for clients for a fee. The result is a "Recollection
Album" consisting of two or three 90 minute cassette
tapes, an edited transcript and a record of family
births, weddings and photos.

728 _____. "Survivors of Holocaust Retell the "Unspeak-
able." **New York Times** September 3, 1979, section
2, p.2. A project in New Haven, Connecticut, supported
by private funds video tapes the recollections of
those who survived World War II in Poland.

Wallechinsky, David, see Medved, Michael.

729 Walls, Dwayne E. **The Kidwells: A Family Odyssey.**
Carolina Academic Press, 1983. Reviewed: **Library
Journal** 108 (December 1, 1983), 2260.

Waltner, John D., see Sprunger, Keith L.

730 Waserman, Manfred J. "Manuscripts and Oral History:
Common Interests and Problems in the History of
Medicine." **Medical Library Association Bulletin** 58
(April 1970), 173-176. The author urges the preservation
of medical history through the taping of oral history.
_____, see also #15.

731 Washington. State Division of Archives and Records
Management. **Oral History Index.** Olympia: State
Printing Plant, 1977.

Watts, Dorothy L., see Frisch, Michael.

732 Wax, Bernard. "The Illinois State Historical Library
Oral History Project." **Illinois Libraries** 45 (February
1963), 92-94. A project of the library aimed at supplementing books and manuscripts in the collection concerning people and events in the state's history is
described.

733 Weart, Spencer R., and David H. DeVorkin. "Interviews
as Sources for History of Modern Astrophysics." **Isis**
72 (September 1981), 471-477. A well-presented account
of the Sources for History of Modern Astrophysics
project by the American Institute of Physics. Four
hundred hours of interviews from one hundred astrono-
mers were taped between 1976 and 1979. Social and

personal aspects were emphasized to supplement written records. The authors describe how interviewees were chosen. An appendix lists the names of interviewees, date of the taping and number of hours of tape recorded.

734 _____, and _____. "The Voice of Astronomical History." **Sky and Telescope** 63 (February 1982), 124-127. A popular presentation of the material from the authors' article which appeared in Isis on the project sponsored by the American Institute of Physics (see above). Photos and two excerpts from interviews with Jesse Greenstein and Martin Schwarzschild are reprinted. The writers take note of some twentieth century controversies in astronomy.

735 Weaver, William J. "Sound Advice: Historical Records." **Modern Photography** 30 (April 1966), 91, 102. An early introduction in a popular vein for the novice.

736 Weber, Arlene. "Mining the Nuggets of the Past or, Oral History Observed." **Journal of Library History** 6 (July 1971), 275-81. Weber's article is an amusing one, based on reminiscences of oral historians at the Fifth Colloquium on Oral History. They recall some of the pitfalls they encountered in various projects.

737 Weber, Devra Anne. "The Organizing of Mexicano Agricultural Workers: Imperial Valley, and Los Angeles 1928-34, An Oral History Approach." **Aztlan** 3 (February 1972), 307-347. Four strikes by Mexican workers are reviewed. Weber sketches the background, discussing links among disputes. The scarcity of material giving the workers' viewpoints led her to use oral history in her research.

Weinberg, Bill, see Shackelford, Laurel.

738 Weitzman, David. "The Gift of History." **American West** 16 (September/October 1979), 16-19, 62-63. With short, undocumented examples of oral history, Weitzman explains the movement for the layperson. He suggests ways for the reader to be his own family historian.

739 Wheelbarger, Johnny J. **Black Religion: A Bibliography of Fisk University Library Materials Relating to Various Aspects of Black Religious Life.** Nashville: 1974. Seven categories of material of interest to those studying the role of religion in the life of blacks are in the university's collection. Interviews with sixteen blacks conducted between 1972 and 1974 are listed.

740 Whipkey, Harry E. "The 1970 Research Conference at Harrisburg: Oral History in Pennsylvania History." **Pennsylvania History** 37 (October 1970), 387-400. An account naming speakers at the conference, their topics and a few lines of description about each.

741 Whitaker, W. Richard. "Why Not Try Videotaping Oral History." **Oral History Review** 9 (1981), 115-124. Videotaping is examined by Whitaker who urges its use for a better all around picture of the interview, especially for its preservation of body language. Equipment and editing of the material are covered. Short bibliography on videotaping.

742 White, George Abbott. "Hem of My Garment: An Interview with Theodore Rosengarten About the Making of Nate Shaw." **Massachusetts Review** 21 (Winter 1980), 787-800. In this interview transcript Rosengarten describes how he went about compiling **All God's Dangers**. See also #593.

743 White, Jerry. **Rothschild Buildings: Life in an East End Tenement Block 1887-1920**. London: Routledge and Kegan Paul, 1980. The oral testimony of 22 people constitutes the main part of the book which centers on the lives of working class Jews in London. Each speaker is identified.

744 Wickman, John E. "An Overview of Oral History." **RQ** 12 (Spring 1973), 290-292. Every project must achieve a balance between what the director would like to do and what is possible with the money available.

745 Widdowson, John D.A. "Oral History and Tradition in an Urban Setting." **Lore and Language** 2, #9 (1978), 43-56.

746 Wilkie, James W. "Alternative Views in History: Historical Statistics and Oral History." In **Research in Mexican History**, Richard E. Greenleaf, and Michael C. Meyer, eds. (Lincoln: University of Nebraska Press, 1973), p.49-62. Wilkie tells how he tried to develop different explanations for Mexico's internal politics by interviewing public officials. He discusses the technical problems in the making and transcribing of the interviews. A partial list of the tapes and their whereabouts is included here. 35 notes with bibliographical references in English and Spanish.

747 _____. "Postulates of the Oral History Center for Latin America." **Journal of Library History** 2 (January 1967), 45-55. The center, housed at Ohio State University, was founded in 1963. For its oral archive on the Mexican Revolution of 1910 interviews are conducted in Spanish. Wilkie lists and briefly discusses eight postulates of oral history. He developed some special techniques for interviewing Latin Americans which take into account that they have a different psychology from natives of the U.S. Short bibliography.

748 _____, and Edna Monzon de Wilkie. "Dimensions of Elitelore: An Oral History Questionnaire." **Journal of Latin American Lore** 1 (Summer 1975), 79-101. The authors reprint here a lengthy questionnaire which they developed for interviewing the political elite of a country. The questions cover general life history and societal views. An appended bibliographic essay suggests directions for further research. _____, see also Brown, Lyle.

749 Williams, Bill. "The Jewish Immigrant in Manchester: The Contribution of Oral History." **Oral History** 7, #1 (1979), 43-53. Williams' interviews document the life of people for whom no written records have been found. He argues that records of other segments of the community give a distorted view of these Jews. The elite were more easily absorbed into English society because they welcomed assimilation.

750 Williams, W.H.A. "They Talk History." **Harvest Years** 12 (March 1972), 32-33. An introductory article urging that projects be undertaken by community organizations.

Winegarden, Mary, see McBane, Margo.

751 Winkler, Karen J. "Transferring Spoken Words to Print: The Problems of the Oral History Book." **Chronicle of Higher Education** 23 (February 14, 1982), 19-20. Using Marjorie Shostak's book **Nisa: The Life and Words of a Kung Woman** as a springboard for discussion, Winkler quotes Grele and Key (q.v.) for their views on editing interviews. Most compilers leave readers in the dark regarding how and what was retained or omitted from a published work. Another problem is what happens to the tapes after publication: are they deposited in a location acessible to scholars, destroyed, or kept by the editor.

752 Winn, Peter. "Oral History and the Factory Study: New Approaches to Labor History." **Latin American Research Review** 14, #2 (1979), 130-140. The author's research centered on a Chilean cotton mill which played a major role in the revolutionary events during the Allende regime. The major part of the article

focuses on the conclusions he reached as a result of interviews with workers. In an appendix Winn discusses what he learned about the methods and techniques of oral history as a result of this project. The best oral historians are those who can empathize with the interviewees while retaining their viewpoints. Ten notes include copious references in English and Spanish.

753 Winstanley, Michael. "Some Practical Hints on Oral History Interviewing." **Oral History** 5 (Spring 1977), 122-130. Winstanley's hints are centered on the equipment: tape recorders, cassettes, the tapes themselves and microphones. He has tips on the actual recording and ways to keep background noises off the tape.

754 Wisconsin. University. River Falls Area Research Center. **Voices from the St. Croix Valley: A Guide to the Oral History Collection.** 2nd ed. River Falls: 1978.

755 Wolkerstorfer, Sister John Christine. "Oral History—A New Look at Local History." **Catholic Library World** 47 (October 1975), 104-107. Sister is director of the oral history project at the College of St. Catherine in St. Paul, Minnesota. She describes how she set up the office and its first eighteen months of operation.

756 _____. "Taping and Tapping a College's Resources." **Catholic Library World** 51 (July 1979), 28-30. An update of the previous article about the development of a collection of material devoted to the history of the college.

757 "Women's History Issue." **Oral History** 5 (Autumn 1977). The issue consists of six articles and a bibliographic essay, all with a British emphasis.

758 "Women's Oral History Resource Section." **Frontiers** 2, #2 (1977), 110-128. The resources are divided by type: a guide with questions to be used for interviewing women; a sample release form; a bibliography of women's oral history; and a guide to American projects by state.

759 Woods, Pendleton. "Living Legends of Oklahoma." **Journal of Library History** 8 (July-October 1973), 167-169. An account of the program conducted by Oklahoma Christian College centering on the history of the state.

760 Woods, Ruby. "From the Pit." **Oral History** 7 (Autumn 1979), 59-62. A life history by the daughter of a Durham, England, miner written in old age.

761 Woodward, Kenneth L. "The Pen Vs. the Tape Recorder."

Newsweek 84 (August 5, 1974), 74-75. A newsy overview of current projects points a finger at the omission of women and blacks from written history. The writer cites opposition by traditional historians to the oral history movement.

762 Workman, Brooke. "Challenges of Oral History." **Clearing House** 46 (February 1972), 380-381. Workman reports on his experiences in using oral history in a high school class. He feels a major result was to awaken students to the relationship between what they learn in class and what happens outside. The school library is the depository for tapes made in class.

763 Wright, George C. "Oral History and the Search for the Black Past in Kentucky." **Oral History Review** 10 (1982), 73-91. Wright deals with three themes: the inadequacy of written sources on black history in Kentucky; major projects being conducted in the state; and some of the problems of the field.

764 Wrigley, Kathryn. **Directory of Illinois Oral History Resources.** Springfield, Ill.: Oral History Office, Sangamon State University, 1981.

765 "Yale to Get Videotaped Interviews with Holocaust Survivors." **New York Times** December 13, 1981, p.62. Tapes made by Laurel Vlock will become part of Yale's Judaica collection. The interviews concentrate on psychological rather than historical aspects of the Holocaust.

766 Yedlin, T. "Documenting Alberta's East European Immigrants." **Canadian Oral History Association Journal** 3, #2 (1978), 29-30.

767 Yocom, Margaret Rose. "Family Folklore and Oral History Interviews: Strategies for Introducing a Project to One's Own Relatives." **Western Folklore** 41 (October 1982), 251-274. Yocom's excellent article points out what many others ignore: some family members may be hostile to the project. She lists ten commandments of family research and suggests way to overcome reticence and/or non-cooperation with examples and excerpts from taped material.

768 _____. "Fieldwork in Family Folklore and Oral History: A Study in Methodology." Doctoral dissertation, University of Massachusetts, 1980. (Dissertation Abstracts 41:1167A). The author outlines research methods she developed to examine the cultural traditions of one's own family. She reviews research on the family and family relationships and concludes with suggestions for carrying out a successful project.

769 Young, Amanda. "Oral History--A Popular Research Technique That Can Work in Music Classes." **Music Educators Journal** 67 (November 1980), 52-55. Standard oral history techniques are listed along with projects specifically aimed at uncovering a group's or individual's musical heritage.

770 Young, Donald Gene. "Appalachian Oral History." **Appalachia** 6 (October-November 1972), 38-39.

771 Yurchenco, Henrietta. **Hablamos! Puerto Ricans Speak Out.** New York: Praeger, 1971. Reviewed: **Library Journal** 97 (July 1971), 2493; **Kirkus Reviews** 39 (October 15, 1971), 1136.

Zabusky, Charlotte F., see Morrison, Joan.

772 Zachert, Martha Jane K. "Implications of Oral History for Librarians." **College and Research Libraries** 29 (March 1968), 101-103. The author lists points which librarians must consider in dealing with oral history materials, touching on their creation, handling, access and methods of bibliographic control.

773 _____. "Sources: Oral History Interviews." **Journal of Library History** 5 (January 1970), 80-87. The major part of the article consists of excerpts from three interviews which illustrate techniques of obtaining information from the subject. The interviewer must have done his homework and be prepared to help the interviewee remember but not censor himself in the process.

Index